Quick Work

Workbook

Michael Duckworth

OXFORD
UNIVERSITY PRESS

OXFORD
UNIVERSITY PRESS

Great Clarendon Street, Oxford OX2 6DP

Oxford University Press is a department of the University of Oxford.
It furthers the University's objective of excellence in research, scholarship,
and education by publishing worldwide in

Oxford New York

Auckland Cape Town Dar es Salaam Hong Kong Karachi
Kuala Lumpur Madrid Melbourne Mexico City Nairobi
New Delhi Shanghai Taipei Toronto

With offices in

Argentina Austria Brazil Chile Czech Republic France Greece
Guatemala Hungary Italy Japan Poland Portugal Singapore
South Korea Switzerland Thailand Turkey Ukraine Vietnam

OXFORD and OXFORD ENGLISH are registered trade marks of
Oxford University Press in the UK and in certain other countries

ACKNOWLEDGEMENTS

The authors and publisher are grateful to those who have given permission
to reproduce the following extracts and adaptations of copyright material:

p7 Information about UPS. Reproduced by permission of UPS (UK).

p11 Extracts from www.tropicalamericantreefarms.com. Reproduced by
permission of Tropical American Tree Farms.

p24 Extracts from www.justdisney.com. Reproduced by permission.

p26 BP logo and information. Reproduced by permission of BP.

p26 Information about Bayer. Reproduced by permission of Bayer Plc.

p26 Information about Peugeot. Reproduced by permission of Peugeot Motor
Company Plc.

p26 Information about Qantas. Reproduced by permission of Qantas Airways

p26 Information about LVMH. Reproduced by permission of LVMH.

p31 Extracts from www.containerstore.com. Reproduced by permission of
The Container Store.

p36 'S-commerce: it might just catch on' by Anna Soderlom. © Times
Newspapers Ltd 24 July 2000. Reproduced by permission of Times
Newspapers Ltd.

p40 '2000 – Irish company of the year'. Appeared in Business and Finance
Magazine. Reproduced by permission of Business and Finance Magazine.

p43 'Tuesday Schmooze'. From NUA Internet Surveys, 29 May 2000.
Reproduced by permission of NUA Ltd.

p50 'Cultural and Cross Border M & A's. From The Antidote Issue 12.
Reproduced by permission of The Antidote.

Sources

p17 Information about Post-it Notes from www.3m.com

p17 Information about Liquid Paper & The Paperclip from
http://inventors.about.com

p17 Information about the Photocopier & Typewriter History from
www.mit.edu

p34 Sainsbury's statistics from J Sainsbury Plc annual review 1999

p34 Emirates Airlines information from http://uaeinteract.com

p44 Career Quiz from www.thoughtfulspot.com

Illustrations supplied by: Nigel Paige, Technical Graphics Dept. OUP p11

Commissioned photography by: Mark Mason p17 (Tippex and Post-it)

*The publisher would like to thank the following for their kind permission to reproduce
photographs*: Bettmann/CORBIS p24; Corbis/N Gunderson p36; J Blair p44
(Crocodile); Mirror Syndication International p46; Ryanair p40; Telegraph
Colour Library/Ryanstock p4; Photomondo p52; The Container Store p31;
Topham/ImageWorks p11; UPS p7; Xerox p17

Designed by: Sarah Tyzack

CONTENTS

1 Exchanging information

1 GETTING INFORMATION

Two business people are talking about their work and their reasons for attending a language course. Put the words in the box in the right order and write the questions in 1–10. See the example.

company do does what your	*are English learning why you*
are for responsible what you	*been English have how long you studying*
are enjoying it you	*based company is the where*
do for who work you	*been for have how long you them working*
do do what you	*are doing course this why you*

1 *Who do you work for?*

I work for Milliken – it's a big private American company.

2 _____?

We manufacture textiles and chemicals.

3 _____?

Our headquarters are in Spartanburg, South Carolina in the USA.

4 _____?

Because it's an American company and most of our meetings are held in English.

5 _____?

I've been studying it for about six months.

6 _____

I'm an accountant with PricewaterhouseCoopers and Lybrand.

7 _____

For the last five years or so.

8 _____

I'm in charge of mergers and acquisitions in Eastern Europe.

9 _____

I need to improve my English and a colleague recommended this course.

10 _____

Yes, I'm having a great time.

2 PRESENT SIMPLE, PRESENT CONTINUOUS, AND PRESENT PERFECT CONTINUOUS

GRAMMAR QUICK CHECK
See pp 53–5

Look at the notes about the uses of the Present simple, Present continuous, and Present perfect continuous. Put the examples from the box in the correct place.

> **Computers _help_ people to work more efficiently.**
> Sorry, you can't speak to the Manager at the moment – he's _talking_ to a client.
> The boss is away this week, so I _am running_ the sales team.
> I've _been working_ for BT for six months.
> We _have_ progress meetings every Monday.
> The Internet _is becoming_ more and more important in business.

– The **Present simple** (_I work, he works_, etc.) is used:

1 to talk about simple facts and things that are permanently true.

Example: _Computers help people to work more efficiently._

2 to talk about regular routines and habits.

Example: _____

– The **Present continuous** (_I am working, she is working, we are working_, etc.) is used:

3 to talk about something that is happening at the moment of speaking.

Example: _____

4 to talk about situations that are temporary rather than permanent.

Example: _____

5 to talk about changes that are taking place over a period of time.

Example: _____

– The **Present perfect continuous** (_I have been working, he has been working_, etc.) is used:

6 to talk about the duration of an activity that began in the past and is still going on. It is often used with _How long …?, for_, and _since_.

Example: _____

3 PRACTICE

This is part of a pre-training form from a Swiss banker to a business English school in Cambridge. Read it and put the verbs in brackets into the Present simple, Present continuous, or Present perfect continuous. See the example.

Please tick ✓ as appropriate	ADDITIONAL COMMENTS
15 What do you feel are your main weaknesses in English? ☐ reading ☐ writing ☐ speaking ☑ listening ☐ other	I _don't have_ (not/have) any problems with reading because I'm familiar with all the technical terms and my written English is OK. I [1]_____ (need) to practise speaking – giving presentations in particular, because my job [2]_____ (change) slowly and I [3]_____ (travel) to England and America more and more. I [4]_____ (think), though, my biggest problem is listening – I often [5]_____ (not/understand) certain words because people – especially native speakers – always [6]_____ (talk) so fast.
16 What kind of language training are you receiving at the moment? ☐ one-to-one lessons ☐ small group lessons ☐ evening classes ☐ self-study ☑ other	Normally the bank [7]_____ (arrange) regular in-company training sessions, and a teacher [8]_____ (come) to the office once a week for a ninety-minute lesson. However, I am now on an assignment in Latvia, and I [9]_____ (set up) a new division here for the last three or four months. As a result, I [10]_____ (not have) any lessons at the moment. But that's OK because most of my colleagues here [11]_____ (come) from all over the world and we all [12]_____ (speak) English together.

4 ON A MISSION

This is an extract from a presentation about UPS. Match the sentences **1–6** with the sentences **a–f** that should follow them. See the example.

1 We have invested a great deal in making our company the most technologically advanced in its sector.

2 We believe in treating every customer with care and respect.

3 We have a reputation for operating fair employment policies.

4 We're committed to taking the best possible care of the environment.

5 We're well known for contributing to charitable and educational community projects.

6 We're proud of being chosen as one of *Fortune* magazine's 'most respected companies'.

a A recent survey placed UPS as the most admired mail package and freight delivery company in the world, and *Forbes* magazine also voted UPS 'Company of the Year'.

b We deliver over 3 billion packages annually, but each customer should feel that their delivery is our top priority.

c The UPS literacy foundation has given nearly $8.5 million to support literacy programmes throughout the country.

d Over the past ten years, we have spent more than $9 billion on information technology, and we continue to spend $1 billion every year.

e UPS has one of the most diverse workforces of any company in the nation. One third of its US workforce of 290,000 is made up of African-Americans, Hispanic-Americans, Asian-Americans and other minorities.

f UPS developed the reusable express envelope, made of 100% recycled fibre. We also carry out research into alternative fuels, and currently UPS has the largest fleet of compressed natural gas (CNG) vehicles in the United States.

5 EXPRESSIONS WITH THE *-ING* FORM

GRAMMAR QUICK CHECK
See p 57

Look at these extracts from the text:

We have invested a great deal **in** *making* …
We believe **in** *treating* …
We have a reputation **for** *operating* …
We're committed **to** *taking* …
We're well known **for** *contributing* …
We're proud **of** *being* …

a What do you notice about the words in *italics*?
b What kind of words are the words in **bold**?

Note: When a verb follows a dependent preposition, it takes the *-ing* form.

6 PRACTICE

Write 6 sentences about your company (or a company you know well) using the words and expressions below. If possible, give examples of what you mean.

1 We have invested a great deal **in** _____

2 We believe **in** _____

3 We have a reputation **for** _____

4 We're committed **to** _____

5 We're well known **for** _____

6 We're proud **of** _____

7 VOCABULARY

Find the adjectives in the wordsearch puzzle that match the definitions below.

1 If a company has high productivity and a small workforce, it is _____. (9)

2 the opposite of public (7)

3 managed in the right way (4–3)

4 growing (9)

5 very energetic (7)

6 If a company loses money, it is _____. (12)

7 This describes a big company that owns a subsidiary. (6)

8 neither very large nor very small (6–5)

9 having offices in many different countries (13)

10 the opposite of modern (3–9)

U	M	E	D	I	U	M	S	I	Z	E	D	E
W	N	R	T	Y	G	J	H	B	D	F	Y	R
E	X	P	A	N	D	I	N	G	F	F	N	W
A	A	P	R	I	V	A	T	E	D	I	A	A
S	L	W	S	O	S	F	R	E	W	C	M	F
A	G	E	F	F	F	E	D	F	R	I	I	G
P	R	L	E	D	R	I	S	D	E	E	C	F
M	U	L	T	I	N	A	T	I	O	N	A	L
S	N	R	V	F	H	T	Y	A	L	T	R	G
W	R	U	P	A	R	E	N	T	B	O	P	U
U	T	N	G	T	F	R	M	N	K	L	F	R
P	O	L	D	F	A	S	H	I	O	N	E	D

8 SET PHRASES: *MAKE* AND *DO*

a Put the words in the box into the correct columns below. See the examples.

a complaint	***military service***	*a job well*	*a suggestion*	*money*
a decision	*some research*	*a lot of damage*	*someone a favour*	
a mistake	*a noise*	*progress*	*an effort*	*the cleaning*	*a phone call*

A *make …*
   a complaint

B *do …*
   military service

b Rewrite the following sentences. Replace the words in *italics* with expressions using *make* or *do*.

1 Do young people in your country have to *join the army*?

Do young people in your country have to *do military service?*

2 I'd better take the car to a mechanic. The engine *is sounding very strange*.

I'd better take the car to a mechanic. The engine is _____ .

3 Before we invest in this project, we need to *find out some more facts*.

Before we invest in this project, we need to _____ .

4 You *were wrong*, so I think you ought to apologize to the customer.

You _____ , so I think you ought to apologize to the customer.

5 Is it OK if I *call someone* from here?

Is it OK if I _____ from here?

6 Could you *help me out*? I need a lift to the airport tomorrow.

Could you _____ ? I need a lift to the airport tomorrow.

7 It's difficult to *become rich* if you don't have any qualifications.

It's difficult to _____ if you don't have any qualifications.

8 The scandal *was very bad* for the company's reputation.

The scandal _____ to the company's reputation.

9 I've been thinking about your problem, and I would like to *propose an idea*.

I've been thinking about your problem, and I would like to _____ .

10 I am writing to *say that I am very dissatisfied* with the poor service I have received.

I am writing to _____ about the poor service I have received.

9 COUNTABLE AND UNCOUNTABLE NOUNS

GRAMMAR QUICK CHECK
See page 57

Uncountable nouns

- are not used with numbers (three, four, etc.)
- take a singular verb form (e.g. *the news **is** good*)
- have no plural form.

Complete the following table showing which words we use with: single countable nouns (e.g. *book*), plural countable nouns (e.g. *books*), and uncountable nouns (e.g. *advice*).

	a book	**b** books	**c** advice
a/an	✓		
six, seven			
my			
the			
this			
these			
how much			
how many			
some			
a little			
a few			
any			

10 PRACTICE

Read these dialogues and choose the correct option from the words in *italics*.

Dialogue 1

A Jane asked me to call you – she said you needed some ¹ *help/helps* with something.

B Yes, I need ² *an/some* advice about getting ³ *a/some* machinery for the printing division.

A What sort of ⁴ *equipment/equipments* are you looking for?

B The main priority ⁵ *is/are* that we need ⁶ *a few/a little* more folding ⁷ *machine/machines*, but at least we've still got a ⁸ *little/few* money left over from last year's budget.

A That's good. Look, leave it with me – I'll do ⁹ *a/some* research and I'll see if I can come up with ¹⁰ *a little/a few* suggestions.

Dialogue 2

A Did you get the ¹ *information/informations* about the latest figures?

B Yes, but the news ² *is/are* bad, I'm afraid.

A What ³ *is/are* the main problem?

B Unemployment ⁴ *is/are* still rising, especially in some ⁵ *area/areas* of the country.

A But there ⁶ *is/are* still plenty of ⁷ *job/jobs* around.

B Yes, but there ⁸ *is very little/are very few* full-time ⁹ *work/works* around. Companies are just not taking on ¹⁰ *much/many* new employees.

11 QUESTION TIME

Read the magazine interview with a farmer who grows tropical trees in Costa Rica. Write down what questions the interviewer probably asked. See the example.

TROPICAL TREE FARMING

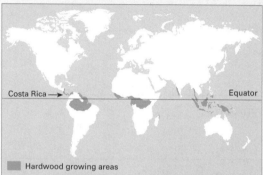

Costa Rica → | Equator

Hardwood growing areas

1 *What line of business are you in?*

We grow tropical trees – mainly teak and other hardwoods – and we have converted seven former cattle ranches in Costa Rica back to tree production.

2 _____

Teak is used for making high quality furniture, cabinets, and expensive boats. Other kinds of tropical hardwood we grow are used for making things like violins and guitars.

3 _____

Yes, and the demand is rising all the time. World consumption of tropical hardwoods is now over 250 million cubic metres, and it is increasing all the time.

4 _____

Yes, the price of teak is rising all the time. It has gone up seven times since 1970, and a single teak log can cost as much as $20,000.

5 _____

At the moment it all comes from natural rainforests. Or nearly all of it does, because only 1% comes from commercial farms. But we must find a solution, because rainforests are important, and if we keep on cutting them down, they will all be gone in thirty-five years.

6 _____

It grows very quickly. And the teak on our farms grows particularly quickly because it is looked after well and there is no competition from other plants.

7 _____

You have to wait about eight years before the first harvest. It's basically a thinning harvest – we take out some of the trees so that the others have more room. For a full-sized tree, you have to wait for about twenty-five years.

12 CHECKING UNDERSTANDING

When we want to check that we have understood something, we often ask a question that repeats the information in a slightly different way. See the example.

1 Over 99% of the world's teak comes from rainforests.

(commercial farms)

So you mean that _less than 1% comes from commercial farms?_

2 A lot of people are giving up cattle farming and going into teak production.

(teak farming/good future)

So you're saying you think that _____?

3 Every year people want more and more teak.

(demand/rise)

So you mean that _____?

4 You can get $1 million for fifty logs.

($20,0000/single log)

So you mean that _____?

5 All the teak will be gone in thirty-five years if we keep on like this.

(do something/replace the teak we use)

So are you saying we _____?

6 A full-sized tree is ready in twenty-five years.

(grow/quickly)

So _____?

13 THE LANGUAGE OF PRESENTATIONS

Put the words in the box in the right order and match them with the words in *italics* that have a similar meaning.

I just saying was as *to let's turn* *about brings me my next point that to*	*as can from graph see this you* *begin I'd like to with* *about be going I'm talking to*

1 *Going back to what I said*, the skills shortage is not going to improve in the short term.

As I was just saying

2 It is clear that training is going to be important for anyone involved in the transportation of these chemicals because they are obviously dangerous. *That raises the issue of* the safety of the workers in the factory.

_____

3 I think I have talked enough about the problems we face in the industry as a whole. Now *I'd like to move on to* some of the solutions that have been proposed.

_____

4 Good morning, ladies and gentlemen. It's great to be here in Zurich and thank you for inviting me. *I've been asked to share some ideas about* ways in which we can improve productivity in the workplace.

_____

5 *As this graph shows*, there has been a steady increase in passenger numbers over the last ten years.

_____

6 *Let's start with* a quick overview of our position in the market.

_____

14 VOCABULARY REVIEW

Read the sentences and choose the correct option to complete them.

1 We expect that you will _____ some mistakes, but you are here to learn.

a do	**b** make	**c** set	**d** be

2 I'd use that company again because I thought they _____ a very good job.

a finished	**b** did	**c** made	**d** took

3 I'm afraid I haven't got my cheque book. Do you _____ credit cards?

a receive	**b** apply	**c** allow	**d** take

4 I'm afraid that the _____ are not very encouraging.

a information	**b** news	**c** facts	**d** advice

5 As everyone is here, let's get _____ .

a starting	**b** beginning	**c** opening	**d** going

6 I am not responsible for distribution, so this problem is not my _____ .

a error	**b** fault	**c** blame	**d** wrong

7 The new software _____ users to create their own web pages easily.

a lets	**b** makes	**c** allows	**d** agrees

8 I'd be happy to _____ questions at the end of my talk.

a reply	**b** take	**c** obtain	**d** admit

9 Could you tell me how much _____ ?

a expensive is the new model	**b** the new model price is
c money is the new model	**d** the new model costs

10 We're famous for _____ reliable cars.

a producing	**b** produced	**c** product	**d** production

2 Sharing ideas

1 MAKING SUGGESTIONS

a Match the sentences **1–6** with sentences **a–f**.

1 Any ideas for lunch?
2 What did you think of the candidates you interviewed?
3 I sent the invoice weeks ago, but they still haven't been paid.
4 I think we need to discuss all this a little more.
5 How could we get more customers to use our website?
6 Shall we use the standard contract?

a We could redesign it and make it easier to use.
b You're right. Why don't we set up another meeting now?
c How about going to that new Thai restaurant?
d I'm not sure – it might be an idea to check that out with the lawyer.
e We'd better send them a reminder.
f Not much. I think we should advertise the vacancy again.

b Rephrase the following, using the words in brackets. See the example.

1 How about meeting for lunch next week?

(should) *We should meet up for lunch next week.*

2 To save some money, we could travel economy class.

(idea) _____

3 I think we should open a branch in Spain.

(Why) _____

4 Why don't you see Mr Jason now and Mr Hayes some other day?

(How) _____

5 It wouldn't be a good idea for us to be late for the meeting.

(better) _____

6 It wouldn't be a good idea for us to offer a bigger discount.

(should) _____

c Using the words and expressions in the box, make suitable suggestions based on the situations below.

> *Why don't you …? You could … How about …? I think you should …*
> *It might be an idea to … You'd better (not) …*

1 Your colleague, who has just had a $3,000 bonus, owes $2,500 on his/her credit card. _____

2 Your colleague has complained that she spends over an hour getting to work every morning. _____

3 A company visitor has asked for ideas about how to spend the evening in your city. _____

4 Your colleague's plane leaves in an hour and a half and he is still at the office. _____

5 Your colleague tells you that everyone in his department is overworked.

_____

6 A company visitor has asked about what sights are worth seeing in your city. _____

2 ACTIVE AND PASSIVE

GRAMMAR QUICK CHECK
See p 56

1 The passive is formed by using the appropriate tense of the verb *to be* and the past participle (e.g. *done, begun, driven,* etc.). For example:
Parts for this car **are made** *in Korea.* (Present simple)
He **was given** *an award for his design.* (Simple past)
They are the only team that **has been trained** *to use the software.* (Present perfect)
They are hoping that they **will be awarded** *the industry prize.* (Future simple)

2 The passive is used to change the focus of a sentence. In passive sentences, the focus is on the verb rather than the person who is performing an action. For example:
A lot of the world's rubber **is grown** *in Malaysia.* (There is no need to add '*by someone/something*'.)

3 When it is important to mention who or what performs the action in the passive, we use *by.*
I feel very sorry for Bill. He has been fired **by** *his new manager.*

4 The passive is often used to talk about systems and processes.
Rubber **is collected** *from the trees two or three times a week, and it* **is taken** *to the factory where it* **is mixed** *with sulphur and* **is heated** *for a long time. This process* **is known** *as vulcanization.*

3 TALKING ABOUT PROCESSES

Read the information about the process of applying for a patent in the United Kingdom. Put the verbs in brackets into the Present simple tense active or passive. See the examples.

Usually, new products _are protected_ (protect) by a patent, which _gives_ (give) the inventor legal rights and safeguards. The stages are as follows:

STAGE 1 PRIOR SEARCH

A search (1)_____ (do) to check that the product (2)_____ (not exist) already, and to check that it will be possible to patent the product. Most of the time searches (3)_____ (carry out) using a computer database, but some companies (4)_____ (do) searches manually.

STAGE 2 INFORMAL APPLICATION

An informal application (5)_____ (sent) to the Patent Office. This (6)_____ (describe) the invention in detail and the product (7)_____ (give) provisional protection for one year.

STAGE 3 FORMAL APPLICATION

With the formal application, details of any new developments (8)_____ (add). The Patent Office (9)_____ (check) its records and (10)_____ (publish) details of the invention.

STAGE 4 EXAMINATION

A year later, the inventor receives a full report giving details of any problems, objections, or legal challenges.

STAGE 5 GRANT

As long as the problems (11)_____ (solve), the patent (12)_____ (grant). As a general rule, the process (13)_____ (take) about 4 years and (14)_____ (cost) £3,300.

4 READING

a   Match the items **1–5** in the pictures to paragraphs **A–E**.

b   Read the paragraphs again. Say if the following statements are true (T) or false (F).

1   Dr Silver came up with the idea of Post-It Notes®. (——)

2   Dr Silver and Art Fry worked for the same company. (——)

3   Bette Nesmith Graham was a pop singer. (——)

4   Bette Nesmith Graham never made a profit from Tippex, (liquid paper). (——)

5   The first typewriter worked very efficiently. (——)

6   The QWERTY arrangement on a typewriter was designed to make typing more difficult. (——)

7   The paper clip was invented in the 13th century. (——)

8   Johan Vaaler was never granted a patent for his invention. (——)

9   Few big companies were interested in Carlson's photocopier. (——)

10   Carlson gave a great deal of his money away. (——)

OFFICE INNOVATIONS

A These use a very weak glue which was discovered accidentally by 3M research scientist Dr Spence Silver. But it was 3M product manager Art Fry who, frustrated by the way bookmarks kept falling out of his books, suddenly realized that Silver's glue could help to make a great bookmark. This led to the new product, and the rest is history.

B This was invented by Bette Nesmith Graham, a single mother who was bringing up her son Michael (who later became a member of the 60s band The Monkees). She got a job as a secretary in the 1950s and hated having to retype letters that had mistakes in them. She made her first batch of her invention at home with her kitchen blender, some paper and some white paint, and went on to make a great deal of money from her product.

C The first of these was made by Christopher Scholes in 1873 and marketed by the Remington Arms company. The early models got jammed if the keys were pressed too quickly. Scholes arranged the letters in such a way that the most common letters were well-spaced. The QWERTY arrangement he eventually chose made typing as difficult and as slow as possible, so the keys had time to fall back before the next letter was pressed.

D In the 13th century, pieces of paper were held together by pieces of string or, later on, waxed ribbons pushed through a hole in the top of the paper. It was 600 years later that Norwegian inventor Johan Vaaler finally came up with a better idea of using a metal pin that was bent in a particular way. He patented the product in 1899, and although others copied and improved his idea, he is thought of as the father of the invention.

E Chester Carlson's job often involved making so many copies of drawings and documents by hand that he decided to try and find a better way. In 1937 he was granted a patent for a process called electrophotography. Sadly, nobody was interested in his idea and he was turned down by companies like IBM, GE and RCA. Eventually the idea was bought and improved by the Haloid company which later changed its name to Haloid Xerox. When Carlson died in 1968, people learnt how generous he had been – of the $150 million he had earned from his invention, he had given $100 million away to charity.

5 PASSIVE REVIEW

Rewrite the following sentences using the passive. Only include the agent (i.e. *by someone*) when it is necessary.

1 People all over the world use Post-It Notes®.

Post-It Notes® _____ all over the world.

2 At the moment they're developing a new generation of mobile phones.

A new generation of mobile phones _____ at the moment.

3 Chester Carlson invented the photocopier.

The photocopier _____ .

4 They've never changed the basic layout of letters on a keyboard.

The basic layout of letters on a keyboard _____ .

5 Inventors should patent any new inventions as soon as possible.

New inventions _____ as soon as possible.

6 Over the next few years, the Internet will transform business and commerce.

Over the next few years, business and commerce _____ .

6 REACTING TO IDEAS

A hotel manager is talking to a colleague. Read the dialogue and choose the best option from the words in *italics*. See the example.

A We need more occupancy at the weekends. And we'd [1] **better**/*must* do something fast because we're losing a lot of money.

B We [2] *shall/could* offer discounts for families, I suppose.

A We tried that [3] *before/ago*, didn't we? It didn't make much difference. We need to target business people.

B Why [4] *don't/not* we offer free rooms on a Saturday night? Completely free. No charge.

A No it [5] *won't/isn't* work. We have to make some money.

B Let me [6] *explain/tell* how it might work. We can make the rooms free but they must have dinner and breakfast in the restaurant.

A It's an interesting [7] *idea/advice* ... and they would probably use other services as well.

B [8] *Why/How* about [9] *to do/doing* it for a month? We can say it's a special deal for our best corporate clients, and get a bit of extra publicity.

A It's worth [10] *a try/to try* – and it's better than having the rooms empty, I suppose.

7 EVALUATING IDEAS

a   Match the sentences **1–4** below with TWO possible endings from **a–h**.

1   I think everyone in the company should take a basic computer course …

_____   _____

2   I think we should introduce flexitime …

_____   _____

3   I'm in favour of this new share option scheme …

_____   _____

4   It's a good idea to have a weekly meeting …

_____   _____

a   it means it will be easier for people to talk about any problems that come up.
b   so people can come in and leave early if they want to.
c   it's going to make everyone feel more committed.
d   then the IT department wouldn't have to waste so much time dealing with simple problems.
e   it means there will be much better communication between the management and the workforce.
f   so people don't always have to travel in the rush hour.
g   that way everyone would know how to use spreadsheets and word processors.
h   it's going to make the staff more interested in the way the company is run.

b   Now complete sentences **1–4** using your own ideas.

8 FIRST AND SECOND CONDITIONALS

GRAMMAR QUICK CHECK
See p 56

1   We use *if* + present tense, *will* + infinitive (the first conditional) to talk about real possibilities and their results.
   *If you **follow** my advice, everything **will be** fine.*
2   We use *if* + past tense, *would* + infinitive (the second conditional), to talk about unlikely or imaginary events and their results.
   *They're talking nonsense. **If** we **followed** their advice, we **would go** out of business in weeks.*
   ***If** I **were** you, I **would proceed** carefully.*

9 PRACTICE

Complete these sentences with the correct form of the verbs in brackets to make first conditional (*if* + present tense / *will* + infinitive) or second conditional (*if* + past tense / *would* + infinitive) sentences.

1 Leave the documents with me. If Mrs Jones _____ (come) in this afternoon, I _____ (give) them to her.

2 I _____ (apply) for that job if I _____ (speak) Spanish, but unfortunately I only speak French.

3 It's a difficult decision, but if I _____ (be) you, I _____ (make) a formal complaint to the manager.

4 I'm sure I _____ (enjoy) work more if I _____ (have) more responsibility, but my boss wants to have complete control over everything.

5 Early retirement is not an option for me. If I _____ (stop) working at 55, I _____ (not/have) enough to live on.

6 _____ (you/keep on) working if you _____ (win) the National Lottery?

7 Please don't bother to come all the way to the airport. If there _____ (not/be) any trains when the plane arrives, I _____ (get) a taxi.

8 Sales are going well, and if we _____ (go) on like this, we _____ (make) a good profit this year.

10 *FOR* AND *AGAINST*

Using the first conditional to promote ideas you like and the second conditional to dismiss ideas you don't like, comment on the following alternatives. See the example.

1 Your company is thinking about relocating 200 miles away. You don't like the idea. Think of one good reason for staying and one big problem with going.
I don't think we should relocate. If we stay where we are, we will be able to carry on business as normal. If we moved 200 miles away, we would lose almost all of our valuable staff.

2 You are advising the government on tax. They are thinking about increasing duty (tax) on petrol by 40%. You are against the idea. Think of one good reason for keeping petrol tax low, and one big problem with increasing tax by 40%.

_____

_____

3 You have a product that is not selling well. You can either try and modify it or start again with a brand new (and much better) product. You want the new

product. Think of one good reason for developing the new product and one big problem with modifying the old product.

_____

_____

4 There is a small stock market crisis, and shares are falling rapidly. An investor wants to sell her shares immediately and take a small loss. You think this is a bad idea. Think of one good reason for holding on to the shares and one big problem with selling them now.

_____

_____

11 VOCABULARY

Complete the puzzle to find a word for an important person in a meeting. All the words come from this unit.

1 CEO stands for Chief _____ Officer.
2 On Wall Street they trade stocks and _____ .
3 A book of instructions or procedures.
4 Don't worry about missing the meeting. I'll be there and I can _____ you in when you get back.
5 Yes, I think you are absolutely right; I _____ with you completely.
6 If you are in charge of security, you are _____ for making sure nothing is stolen.
7 We'd _____ go now or we'll be late.
8 It's not _____ trying to get her to change her mind. It'll never work.
9 The process of generating lots of ideas as a group.
10 Most of the problems we had were brought _____ by a lack of communication.
11 A list of things to be discussed in a meeting.

12 THE LANGUAGE OF MEETINGS

a Read these short extracts that come from different stages in a meeting. Put the extracts **A–F** into the correct order **1–6**.

1 _____ 2 _____ 3 _____ 4 _____ 5 _____ 6 _____

A

ANNA OK, so we have agreed that there will be security cameras and alarms on the fire exits, and everyone will come in and leave through the main entrance.

BILL And there will always be a security guard.

ANNA That's right.

B

DIANE   … lovely beaches, clean seas, and there's a great little restaurant just near the hotel.

ANNA   Thank you, Diane. Perhaps we could go back to that later if we have time. We need to look at the next item on the agenda, which is improving security arrangements. What exactly is the problem at the moment?

BILL   In the last three months, we've lost more than fifteen top quality PCs. Someone is just walking off with them …

C

DIANE   Are we finished then?

ANNA   Yes, I think so. Is there anything else that anyone wants to say? OK, we'll meet again next Friday at 10.30.

D

ANNA   So you are against the idea of locking the other exits?

BILL   Absolutely – I'm quite sure it would break the fire regulations even if it did stop people from stealing computers.

ANNA   How do you feel about this, Diane?

DIANE   I think Bill's right as far as the law goes, and there must be a better way …

E

ANNA   Thank you all for coming. Now, before we start, could I remind everyone that I'm aiming to get through this by 3.30?

BILL   Will we have enough time?

ANNE   Yes, I certainly hope so as long as we keep to the agenda.

F

ANNA   Let's turn to the first item on the agenda, which is sickness pay for part-time employees. Bill, you have looked into this – could you fill us in on what you have found out?

BILL   Yes, I've talked to the company lawyers and one of the union representatives, and I'm pretty sure we won't have a repeat of last year's problems. Basically we have agreed …

b What is the name of the person chairing the meeting?

_____

c In which extract (**A–F**) is the chairperson:

1 setting a time when the meeting should end? ____

2 summarizing the decisions that have been made? ____

3 asking for different opinions? ____

4 getting the discussion back on to the topic? ____

5 formally finishing the meeting? ____

6 introducing the first topic for discussion? ____

Tackling problems

1 READING

Read the text and complete it with the Simple past or the past participle of the irregular verbs in brackets. See the examples.

WALT DISNEY, one of the great figures of 20th century cinema, was born in Chicago in 1901. The family soon moved to a farm in Missouri, where Walt 1 _spent_ (spend) much of his childhood. He showed a talent for art from an early age, and sometimes 2 _sold_ (sell) drawings and sketches that he had 3 _____ (do) to neighbours to earn a little extra money.

He tried to enlist for military service in 1918, but was turned down because of his age. Instead, he joined the Red Cross, who 4 _____ (send) him to France as an ambulance driver. On his return, he 5 _____ (begin) making short animated films for local businesses in Kansas, but moved to Hollywood to join his brother Roy because his company Laugh-o-Grams had 6 _____ (go) bankrupt.

Walt and Roy 7 _____ (set) up a new company in Hollywood, and their reputation 8 _____ (grow) rapidly. Walt created a new character *Mickey Mouse* in 1928, who appeared in *Steamboat Willie* just as sound was becoming more common in movies. He had an endless drive to perfect the art of animation, and 9 _____ (hold) the patent for Technicolor for two years, allowing him to make the only colour cartoons.

In 1937, the full-length feature *Snow White and the Seven Dwarfs* 10 _____ (catch) the public's imagination and was an instant success. It had 11 _____ (cost) $1,499,000 – an amazing amount of money, as many businesses were still feeling the effects of the Depression, but the film is still considered one of the greatest achievements of the motion picture industry.

Over the next few years, Walt Disney Studios 12 _____ (bring) out other full-length classics such as *Pinocchio, Dumbo* and *Bambi*.

Walt's dream of a clean and well-organized amusement park 13 _____ (come) true when Disneyland opened in 1955, and Disney began TV production in 1961.

The company continued to expand after Walt Disney's death in 1966, and 14 _____ (build) additional theme parks and film and TV studios. Recently, under CEO Michael Eisner, it has developed a significant Internet presence and the company is now ranked as the third largest media conglomerate in the world with annual sales of over $20 billion.

2 SIMPLE PAST, PAST CONTINUOUS, AND PAST PERFECT

GRAMMAR QUICK CHECK
See pp 53–5 and p 59

1   We use the **Simple past** to refer to past actions that happened one after the other.
*Disneyland **opened** in 1955, and Disney **began** TV production in 1961.*

2   We use the **Past continuous** to talk about something that was already in progress at a point of time in the past.
*Disney created Mickey Mouse just as sound **was becoming** more common in movies.*

3   We use the **Past perfect** to show that one past action was completed before another past action.
*Disney moved to Hollywood because his first company **had gone** bankrupt.*

3 PRACTICE

a   Complete the sentences by putting one of the verbs in brackets into the Simple past and the other into the Past continuous.

1   The new secretary _got_ into trouble because she _was using_ the company phone to make personal calls. (use, get)

2   I first _____ Anna when I _____ a training course in Chicago. (meet, attend)

3   Some of the files _____ lost while we _____ into our new offices. (get, move)

4   They _____ to stop production of the old model because it _____ well. (decide, not sell)

5   What _____ when I _____ this morning? (you/do, call)

6   The accountant _____ a serious error while she _____ the accounts. (notice, check)

b   Complete these sentences in two ways with a verb:
–   in the Past continuous to talk about background actions and activities
–   in the Simple past to talk about what happened next. See the example.

1   When the company went out of business …
a   _we were losing $1 million a month._
b   _everyone lost their job._

2   When I phoned Jack …
a   _____
b   _____

3   When I was offered my present job …
a   _____
b   _____
c   _____

4 COMPANY HISTORIES

a Read these extracts **A–E** from company histories and match them with the companies in **1–5**.

b Put the verbs in brackets into the Simple past (e.g. *did*) or Past perfect (e.g. *had done*).

A In 1908, English explorer William Knox Darcy [1] _____ (found) Anglo-Persian to exploit the vast oil reserves that he [2] _____ (discover) in the Middle East. Winston Churchill persuaded the British government to buy a fifty-one per cent share in Anglo-Persian in 1914.

B One of the companies in this multi-billion dollar group operated primarily as a wholesaler of luggage until 1977 when Henry Racamier, an ex-steel executive who [3] _____ (marry) into the Vuitton family, [4] _____ (take) charge. Under Racamier, sales soared from $20 million to almost $1billion within ten years.

C The company's research labs [5] _____ (allow) it to grow rapidly beyond the synthetic dye business that it [6] _____ (start) as originally. Some of its major breakthroughs were Antinonin, (first synthetic pesticide, 1892), aspirin (1899), and synthetic rubber (1915).

D In 1976, the French government [7] _____ (persuade) the company to merge with Citroën, which Andre Citroën [8] _____ (set) up in 1915, and in 1919 had become the first in Europe to mass-produce cars.

E In 1920, Hudson Fysh and Paul McGuinness, who [9] _____ (fight) together as pilots in the First World War, [10] _____ (create) the Queensland and Northern Territory Aerial Services to link Darwin and Queensland. By 1930 it had expanded enormously, with air routes stretching from Darwin and Brisbane to the Coral Sea.

Tackling problems

5 CAUSES AND RESULTS

Using your own ideas, complete these sentences in two different ways:
- *because* + Past perfect to talk about causes
- *so* + Simple past to talk about results.

See the example.

1 The major shareholders were angry …

because the company had performed badly.

so they voted for a new chairman.

2 I was late for the meeting …

because _____ .

so _____ .

3 They narrowly failed to win the contract …

because _____ .

so _____ .

4 He contacted the IT department urgently …

because _____ .

so _____ .

5 In the restaurant, she refused to pay the bill …

because _____ .

so _____ .

6 They couldn't take the plane to Paris …

because _____ .

so _____ .

GRAMMAR QUICK CHECK
See pp 53–4

6 PRESENT PERFECT AND SIMPLE PAST

1 We often use the Present perfect when there is a link between the past and the present.
*I'm afraid Mr Jacobs isn't here today. He **has gone** to London.*

2 The Present perfect is often used with *ever, never, already,* and *(not) yet* in sentences where the time period is not finished (*today, so far this week, this month,* etc.).
*So far this morning I**'ve already been** to two meetings but I haven't opened my mail yet. (The morning isn't finished yet.)*
***Have** you **ever been** to Japan? (i.e. in all your life up to now)*

3 The Simple past is used to talk about past events in finished time periods.
*The meeting **went** well yesterday.*

4 The Present perfect is NOT used with past time expressions like *yesterday, at 5.15, last month, on June 25th, in 1988,* etc.

7 TALKING ABOUT CURRENT PROBLEMS

Write down how you could rephrase the problems below. Use the Present perfect (*have done, has done,* etc.) and the verbs in brackets. See the example.

1 The photocopier isn't working.

(break down) *The photocopier has broken down.* _____

2 I'm afraid you are too late to catch the flight.

(miss) _____

3 I'm afraid your tickets aren't here yet.

(not/arrive) _____

4 My keys are missing.

(lose) _____

5 There aren't any more catalogues.

(run out of) _____

6 Our website has a new design.

(redesign) _____

7 It isn't raining any more.

(clear up) _____

8 Twenty people from the IT department are now unemployed.

(make redundant) _____

8 SIMPLE PAST OR PRESENT PERFECT?

Put the verbs in brackets into the Simple past or Present perfect.

1 Sales are going well this year and we _____ (already/reach) our targets.

2 Mr Lawson _____ (join) the company in 1998.

3 This package _____ (come) for you yesterday.

4 _____ (you/ever/work) for a large organization?

5 She's working as hard as she can on the report but she _____ (not/finish) it yet.

6 So far this year a lot of new Internet companies _____ (go) out of business.

7 I _____ (not/speak) to Miss Hoover this morning, but I'll try and see her some time this afternoon.

8 What is the new publicity brochure like? I _____ (not/see) it yet.

9 The meeting _____ (break) up at 12.30.

10 We _____ (spend) far too much on business travel last year.

9 DISCUSSING MISTAKES

A manager is talking to a junior colleague about a marquee (i.e. a large tent used for social events) that she has hired for a conference. Read the dialogue and complete the exercise that follows.

A   How much was the marquee?

B   It came to £8,900.

A   That seems very high. How come?

B   Well, I just phoned up the company – they told me how much it would cost and I agreed to it.

A   It's a pity you didn't try to get a better deal. You were wrong to accept a quote like that. What company did you use?

B   Sandringham Marquees.

A   Oh, them. It would have been better to use Hamlin Hire. They're much cheaper.

B   I'm sorry – it was a mistake for me not to ask you first.

A   Anyway, when are they coming to put it up? They're leaving it a bit late, aren't they?

B   Yes, they were supposed to put it up yesterday, but it was too big for their van.

A   Why on earth didn't they think of that before?

B   I don't know, but I think I ought to give them a call. They were meant to phone me this morning to arrange a time, but they haven't rung yet.

Rephrase these extracts from the dialogue using *should have* or *shouldn't have*. See the example.

1   It's a pity you didn't try to get a better deal.

You should have tried to get a better deal.

2   It would have been better to use Hamlin Hire.

_____

3   You were wrong to accept a quote like that.

_____

4   It was a mistake for me not to ask you first.

_____

5   They were supposed to put it up yesterday.

_____

6   Why on earth didn't they think of that before?

_____

7   They were meant to phone me this morning.

_____

10 *MUST, MUSTN'T, OR NEEDN'T*

After the problem with the marquee, the manager has sent the following memo to new members of staff. Complete the memo with *must, needn't,* or *must not*.

MEMO

To: All new staff members at C, D, and E Grade
From: Frank Harris
cc: LPG, TD
Re: Ordering goods and services

I am writing to clarify the position on ordering goods and services on behalf of the company for staff at C, D, and E Grades.

If you are a member of staff at Grade E, you ¹ _____ agree to purchase anything at all. Instead you ² _____ refer any spending requirements to a Junior Manager (Grade D) in your department who will make the decision.

If you are a Junior Manager (Grade D), you may make spending decisions for yourself and Grade E staff, and as long as the amount is less than €5,000, you ³ _____ refer to an Executive Manager (Grade C). However, you ⁴ _____ refer any decisions over €5,000 to a Grade C Manager. In addition, you ⁵ _____ keep strictly within your budget and you ⁶ _____ exceed your quarterly spending targets under any circumstances.

---

11 VOCABULARY: *SAY* AND *TELL*

Complete these sentences with the correct form of *say* or *tell*.

1   I'm sorry, I didn't hear that. Could you _____ it again?

2   It's sometimes difficult to _____ the difference between a real banknote and a fake.

3   I'll call you back in a minute. Could you _____ me your number?

4   I'm very sorry to hear your news. Christina _____ me what happened.

5   Excuse me, could you _____ me what the time is?

6   At the meeting, the CEO _____ that the company had had a very successful year.

7   In interviews you must be honest and _____ the truth about qualifications and so on.

8   Could you _____ me when the next train leaves?

12 VOCABULARY

Unscramble the letters in brackets to complete the text. Each correct answer begins with the letter in bold. See the example.

THE BEST company to work for in America

THE CONTAINER STORE, which sells boxes and shelving and other storage items, was recently voted number 1 in *Fortune* magazine's list of the '100 Best Companies to Work for in America.' The company beat (1) _giants_ (**g**aint s) such as Southwest Airlines, Microsoft and Intel, so what is it that makes this relatively small company such a special (2) _____ (**e**rlmopey)?

Certainly, employees at the Container Store are (3) _____ (**e**deilntt) to a good range of (4) _____ (**b**eefints). They receive excellent (5) _____ (**t**agiinnr) and their (6) _____ (**s**aaeilrs) are higher than the industry average. One of the (7) _____ (**p**ekrs) is a 40% (8) _____ (**d**cinostu) on company products, and there is a profit (9) _____ (**s**aghinr) scheme for the (10) _____ (**s**afft).

However, what makes the Container Store different is its corporate (11) _____ (**c**elrtuu). The company sees its employees as its greatest (12) _____ (**a**esst) and values them to a high degree. It goes to great lengths to (13) _____ (**r**ceirut) not just good people, but great people, and that is one of the secrets of the company's success. Employees are (14) _____ (**e**cadegnoru) to use their own intuition and creativity to solve (15) _____ (**p**belmors) and don't have to follow a rule book. There is also a profound level of (16) _____ (**c**aciimmnnootu) within the company and details of everything from daily sales, (17) _____ (**b**degstu) and expansion plans are shared with everyone. This gives them a great sense of ownership, and staff (18) _____ (**t**enorruv) is extremely low.

As the President of the company says: 'A funny thing happens when you take time to educate your employees, pay them well and treat them as (19) _____ (**e**alqsu). You end up with extremely (20) _____ (**m**adeiottv) and enthusiastic people.'

13 RULES AND REGULATIONS

a Write sentences about what you or other people where you work have to do or don't have to do. Use the verbs in the list. See the example.

| have to | don't have to | can/allowed to | can't/not allowed to |

1 work five days a week

I have to work five days a week.

2 wearing a uniform

3 work 9 a.m. to 5 p.m.

4 work overtime

5 attend meetings

6 smoke

b Using your own ideas, write five more sentences about the rules where you work using the verbs in the box.

14 CHANGING PLANS

Read the phone conversation and choose the best options from the words in *italics*. See the example.

A Ann Langton.
B Good morning, Mrs Langton. ¹ **This**/*Here* is Klaus Bauer from Tricolor Clothing.
A Hi, how ² *can/shall* I help you?
B I'm calling ³ *over/about* our meeting on Tuesday. I'm afraid that something's ⁴ *gone/come* up and I won't be able to ⁵ *make/come* it.
A That's OK. ⁶ *Do/Would* you like to fix another date?
B Yes, that would be great.
A How are you ⁷ *arranged/fixed* for Thursday?
B I'm ⁸ *busy/occupied* in the morning. Would you mind to ⁹ *meet/meeting* in the afternoon?
A No problem. Let's ¹⁰ *say/tell* 3.30?
B That's ¹¹ *well/fine* for me.
A Would you like ¹² *me/for me* to bring some samples?
B If you could, that would be great because you get a much better idea than just looking at the catalogue. By the way, do you mind ¹³ *if/when* I bring a colleague along to the meeting?
A ¹⁴ *No/Yes* – that's fine by me.
B OK. See you on Thursday, then. Goodbye.
A Goodbye.

15 REQUESTS, OFFERS, AND INVITATIONS

Rewrite the sentences using the word in brackets. See the example.

1 Do you want me to send you the latest price list?

Would *you like me to send* you the latest price list? (me)

2 Would it be inconvenient for you to come to my office instead?

Would _____ to my office instead? (mind)

3 May I come in late tomorrow?

Do _____ in late tomorrow? (mind)

4 Do you want to arrange a time to have lunch?

Would _____ a time to have lunch? (like)

5 Could you bring the files with you?

Would _____ the files with you? (mind)

6 Do you want to cancel the order?

Would _____ the order? (like)

16 POLITELY DOES IT

Using the phrases in the box, write down what you would say in each of the situations below.

> *I'm afraid that …*
> *Excuse me, do you know if …*
> *Excuse me, could you tell me when …*
> *I'm sorry, I'm terribly busy at the moment. Would you mind …*
> *Could you tell me how …*

1 You are at the train station in Tokyo but do not understand the timetable. You want information about the time of the next train for Kyoto.

_____

2 A colleague has come to see you, but you are too busy to talk to her at the moment. Ask her to come back later.

_____

3 You are in a strange city and someone asks you for directions. Explain that you don't know the city.

_____

4 You are at the airport. Is there a cash machine nearby? Ask someone.

_____

5 You are on the London underground and cannot work out how to get to Olympia from the station you are at. Ask someone.

_____

4

Planning ahead

1 TALKING ABOUT PLANS

a Match **1–4** of these newspaper extracts about company plans to **A–D**.

1 _____
2 _____
3 _____
4 _____

1 This year Sainsbury's opened 20 new supermarkets.

2 Emirates Airlines have ordered five of Airbus Industries' new double-decker super-jumbos, which will be capable of carrying 555 passengers.

3 The Turkish government intends to build a major dam in the south east to generate electricity as it wants to reduce its use of fossil fuels.

4 According to industry sources, Nalso Pharmaceuticals is about to announce promising results from studies on its new anti-viral drug Vaxifan.

A It is hoping to carry out clinical trials shortly with a view to starting production next year, but some analysts doubt they will be able to get FDA approval for the new medicine so quickly.

B The first flight is expected to take place in four years, and delivery of the order is due the following year.

C Next year, it will continue to expand, and it is planning to open a further 15 stores with a total sales area of 386,000 sq ft.

D It has told opponents that it is going to relocate some of the most important structures of the town of Hasankeyf which will be submerged when the new lake is formed.

b From the letters in the wordsnake, find all the words and expressions from the texts that were used to express thoughts about the future. See the example.

willisplanningtoisexpectedtoisdueintendstowantstoisgoingtoisabouttoishopingtodoubt

1 _will_   5 _____   8 _____
2 _____   6 _____   9 _____
3 _____   7 _____   10 _____
4 _____

2 PLANS AND INTENTIONS

Using some of the expressions from exercise1, comment on the following topics. Say what you do/don't hope, plan, or intend to do. See the example.

1 promotion
I am due to get promoted soon.

2 position at work

3 retirement age

4 travel abroad

5 salary

6 further courses/education

7 moving house

8 responsibilities at work

9 changing jobs

3 QUIZ: FAMOUS WRONG PREDICTIONS

Read through the list of wrong predictions and see if you can match the ideas **1–7** with the speakers **a–g**. It goes to show how difficult it can be to look into the future.

1 There is not the slightest indication that nuclear energy will ever be obtainable. ____

2 Stocks have reached what seems like a permanently high plateau. ____

3 Who the hell wants to hear actors talk? ____

4 I think there is a world market for maybe five computers. ____

5 We don't like their sound, and guitar music is on the way out. ____

6 640K ought to be enough for anybody. ____

7 Louis Pasteur's theory of germs is ridiculous fiction. ____

a 1872: Pierre Pacher, Professor of Physiology at Toulouse
b 1927: H. M. Warner, founder of Warner Brothers
c 1929: Irving Fischer, Professor of Economics, Yale University
d 1932: Albert Einstein
e 1943: Thomas Watson, Chairman of IBM
f 1962: Decca Recording Co, rejecting the Beatles
g 1981: Bill Gates, Microsoft

4 TALKING ABOUT PROBABILITIES

Read the text and complete the exercise that follows.

S-COMMERCE
THE NEXT BEST THING?

YOU'VE HEARD OF **E-COMMERCE**, you may even have heard of m-commerce (Internet transactions over a mobile phone), but it seems there is a new buzz word that Internet retailers *definitely won't* be able to ignore for long – it's S-commerce. That's 'shops' to you and me.

'It's a revelation,' says one reporter. 'You just walk into one of these "shops" and they have all sorts of things for sale.' Particularly impressive, apparently, was a clothes shop discovered while **browsing** in Central London. 'Shops seem to be the ideal medium for transactions of this type,' says one spokesman, 'and they *are likely to* become more and more popular.'

One of the big advantages of the shop is that customers can actually try something on and see if it fits. This is made possible by using a **high-definition** 2-D viewing system, or 'mirror' as it has become known. 'Sometimes,' says one shopper, 'I don't have time to **download** huge Flash **animations** of rotating Nikes and then wait five days for someone to deliver a pair that *probably won't* fit.'

Shops, which are frequently aggregated into physical shopping **portals** or 'high streets', are becoming increasingly popular with the cash-rich, time-poor generation of new consumers. By concentrating distribution to a series of high-volume outlets in urban centres – typically close to where people live and work – businesses *will certainly* be able to make dramatic savings. This new method of distribution is far more efficient than the wasteful practice of delivering items one-by-one to people's homes.

We reckon S-commerce *could* have a serious future, and we haven't heard the last of it yet.

a In the text, the writer uses a number of words and phrases that are often used when talking about computers or the Internet. Find a word or phrase in **bold** that means:

1 looking around _____

2 large sites _____

3 to receive files and data from the Internet _____

4 moving pictures or illustrations _____

5 very clear _____

b The writer makes a number of predictions in the text. Find a word or phrase in *italics* from the text that means the same as:

1 are certainly not going to _____

2 aren't likely to _____

3 might _____

4 are probably going to _____

5 are definitely going to _____

5 THE LANGUAGE OF PREDICTIONS: PRACTICE

Rewrite these sentences using the word in brackets. See the example.

1 There is absolutely no chance of the company making a profit this year.
The company *definitely won't make a profit this year.* (definitely)

2 There is no doubt that companies will develop alternatives to petrol.
Companies _____ . (certainly)

3 Millions of people are probably going to lose their jobs because of new technology.
Millions of people _____ . (likely)

4 There's a chance of interest rates rising later in the year.
Interest rates _____ . (might)

5 Most analysts believe that this latest takeover bid probably won't succeed.
Most analysts believe that this latest takeover bid _____ . (likely)

6 WRITING

Using your own ideas, write short paragraphs giving your opinions about what you think will happen in the future. Make predictions about:

1 the kind of money people will/won't use

_____

_____

2 traditional businesses and new Internet companies

_____

_____

3 changes in the workplace and working routines.

_____

_____

7 TALKING ABOUT PRICES

a Match the words and phrases in the list with the graphs. Some graphs have more than one matching word or phrase.

climbed steadily	rocketed	crashed
rose dramatically	fell dramatically	fell gradually
went up gradually	fluctuated wildly	

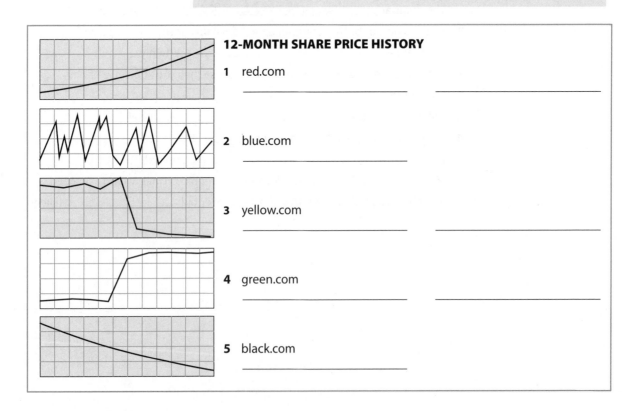

12-MONTH SHARE PRICE HISTORY

1 red.com

_____   _____

2 blue.com

_____

3 yellow.com

_____   _____

4 green.com

_____   _____

5 black.com

_____

b Using the information in the text, complete the graph showing the twelve-month share price history.

IN JANUARY, the shares started at 50p, and climbed steadily, ending up at 65p in February. Following some disappointing results, they fell gradually until they reached 45p in April. When the company announced plans for the new Internet division, it became the centre of intense media interest. The shares fluctuated wildly, hitting a high of 90p in May and July and lows of 20p in June and August. In September, however, shares rose by 10p and in October grew by a further 15p. After talk of a possible takeover bid, shares rocketed and ended up at £1.05 in November. This did not take place, and when the company was raided by the Serious Fraud Office and the Chairman was accused of theft and false accounting, the shares went through the floor and trading was suspended when the shares fell to 5p in December.

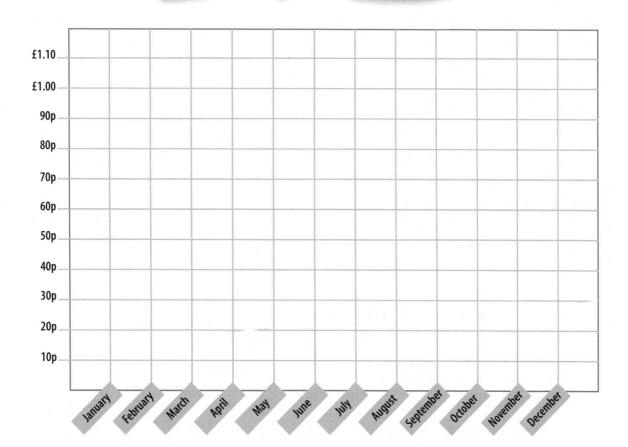

8 READING

a Read the text about the low-cost airline Ryanair. Unscramble the letters in brackets to make two-part adjectives. Each answer begins with the letter in bold. See the example.

STRENGTHS AND WEAKNESSES

RYANAIR, the airline run by Michael O'Leary, is one of Ireland's most successful and dynamic companies and is now Europe's largest and most profitable (1) _low-fares_ (olw-raefs) carrier. Last year it carried 7 million passengers, making it bigger than the national carrier Aer Lingus, and this year it will make nearly £70 million in (2) _____-_____ (re**p**-xat) profits.

When the airline began 15 years ago, the main route was from Dublin to London Stansted. The airport is badly positioned for many people in the UK, but passenger numbers were reasonable because the fares were so low. However, the airline had to fight very hard to survive and made some powerful enemies along the way. Worries about safety and mishandling of passenger complaints gave the company a rather poor public image of being aggressive and (3) _____-_____ (**d**won-kmerta), and it has still not fully recovered from this.

In other countries where Ryanair has opened new routes, particularly in Italy, it is extremely popular. It offers a wide range of flights at about 20% of the traditional (4) _____-_____ (**h**gih-mngira) Alitalia fare, and O'Leary hopes that there will be (5) _____-_____ (glare-lcsae) expansion into Europe. There is plenty of room for growth, although there will also be more competition from other (6) _____-_____ (tcu-cpire) airlines like Easyjet, Buzz or Go. 'Less than 1% of intra-European travel is carried by low fares airlines at the moment, whereas the US figure is nearer to 15%. There's no reason why, if we remain a (7) _____-_____ (llew-nmagaed) group, we can't be carrying 20 to 25 million passengers within ten years and even overtake British Airways.'

The (8) _____-_____ (sfat-whtgro) world of the Internet is already playing a role in the way the company is developing. The Ryanair website accounts for 20% of bookings and has allowed the company to cut costs by £10 million. In addition, as the website is the most popular one in Ireland, it generates a further £10 million in advertising.

As O'Leary points out, running any airline company is a risky business. An air crash could have a very damaging effect, and changes in EU or government regulations, such as the ending of (9) _____-_____ (ty**d**u-eerf) sales, can have a big effect on profits. Even so, the future looks promising, and the airline has a good chance of achieving its (10) _____-_____ (lgno-mret) growth plans.

b Read the text again and complete a SWOT analysis on Ryanair. Make your notes in the boxes below.

STRENGTHS	WEAKNESSES
OPPORTUNITIES	THREATS

9 IF, WHEN, IN CASE, UNLESS, UNTIL

Complete the example sentences **a–e** in the list with *if, when, in case, unless,* or *until* and write them in the correct place **1–5** in the notes below.

> *a* I'm coming to London next week – I'll give you a call _____ I get there.
> *b* There's a chance I may be coming to London next week. _____ I do decide to come, I'll let you know.
> *c* I have insured the jewellery _____ it gets lost or stolen.
> *d* I'll assume the meeting is going ahead as planned _____ I hear from you otherwise.
> *e* He's sixty-three now, so he'll carry on working here _____ he retires.

1 We use *if* to talk about a future event that may or may not take place.

Example: _____

2 We use *when* to talk about a future event that we are sure will take place.

Example: _____

3 *Unless* is similar in meaning to *if … not*.

Example: _____

4 We use *until* to talk about something that will happen between now and a point of time in the future.

Example: _____

5 We use *in case* to talk about precautions and things that might happen.

Example: _____

10 PRACTICE

a Rewrite these sentences using the words in brackets. See the example.

    1 I always take my cell phone because I might need to call the office.

         I always take my cell phone _in case I need to call the office._ (in case)

    2 Only sign the contract if the lawyers have had a good look at it.

         Don't sign the contract _____ . (unless)

    3 We will only make a profit if we sell more than 100,000 units.

         We _____ . (unless)

    4 When I have finished my work I'll go home.

         I won't _____ . (until)

    5 I will get to London. Then I will phone you.

         I will _____ . (when)

    6 They may offer me the job. I will accept it.

         I will _____ . (if)

    7 We need to sort out these problems and then we'll be on schedule.

         We'll be on schedule _____ . (if)

    8 I will only go back to work when the strike is over.

         I won't go back _____ . (until)

    9 He's going to call in. I will give him your message then.

         I'll give him your message _____ . (when)

   10 Take some local currency with you. The banks may be shut when you get to Moscow.

         Take some local currency with you _____ . (in case)

b Complete each of these sentences in five different ways. See the example.

1 I'm going to study English …

    a if _I can find classes._ _____

    b when _____

    c until _____

    d unless _____

    e in case _____

2 I'm going to stay at the office …

    a if _____

    b when _____

    c until _____

    d unless _____

    e in case _____

Planning ahead

11 VOCABULARY

Read the text and fill the gaps with the best option **a–d** below. See the example.

FIRST TUESDAY

So, what are you doing next Tuesday evening? Chances are, if you're trying to get an Internet 1 _start-up_ off the ground, you'll be at a First Tuesday meeting. From Bratislava to Buenos Aires, the First Tuesday club hosts meetings where entrepreneurs can pitch to 2 _____ capitalists on the first Tuesday of every month.

■ The founders 3 _____ the idea of the club when a few journalists and financial whiz-kids decided to try and recreate a Silicon valley style 4_____ event in the UK. It now has over 20,000 members in London alone and a further 50,000 scattered in more than 50 countries around the world. The club aims to help high-tech entrepreneurs 5 _____ access to capital, management, staff and other resources.

■ At First Tuesday meetings, investors wear red dots, entrepreneurs wear green dots and journalists wear yellow dots. After an opening speech, the fun begins as the green dotters swarm around the red dotters and the yellow dotters take notes like 6 _____ .

■ If the entrepreneurs make a good impression, investors will ask for more meetings 7 _____ they are satisfied that the entrepreneurs have sufficient skills to 8 _____ deadlines and run a project 9 _____ budget. They will also need to explain who the 10 _____ customers will be, how they will 11 _____ them and will probably need to be prepared to give up some or most of the 12 _____ in exchange for finance.

■ First Tuesday is apparently 13 _____ its own advice and planning an *IPO. Julie Meyer, one of the co-founders, has said on a number of 14 _____ that First Tuesday is going to be 'a billion dollar company'. And, it must be said, one that is 15 _____ to fail.

*IPO: initial public offering

1	**a** beginner	**b** debutante	**c** start-up	**d** apprentice
2	**a** investment	**b** finance	**c** funding	**d** venture
3	**a** hit up	**b** hit at	**c** hit down	**d** hit on
4	**a** frameworking	**b** networking	**c** teleworking	**d** homeworking
5	**a** beat	**b** win	**c** gain	**d** advance
6	**a** crazy	**b** quickly	**c** madly	**d** busily
7	**a** until	**b** during	**c** in case	**d** without
8	**a** finish	**b** achieve	**c** meet	**d** succeed
9	**a** inside	**b** beneath	**c** behind	**d** within
10	**a** incoming	**b** potential	**c** capable	**d** thinkable
11	**a** reach	**b** touch	**c** attain	**d** call
12	**a** equity	**b** equation	**c** equivalence	**d** equipment
13	**a** making	**b** having	**c** doing	**d** taking
14	**a** chances	**b** possibilities	**c** occasions	**d** opportunities
15	**a** uncertain	**b** unsure	**c** indefinite	**d** unlikely

Planning ahead

Resolving conflict

1 QUIZ

This humorous quiz consists of four questions that tell you whether or not you are qualified to be a professional. See the results at the end of the quiz.

THE CAREER QUIZ

The answers are upside down below the picture. There is no need to cheat. The questions are not that difficult. You just need to think like a professional.

1 How do you put a giraffe into a refrigerator?

Correct answer: Open the refrigerator, put in the giraffe and close the door. This question tests whether or not you tend to do simple things in a complicated way.

2 How do you put an elephant into a refrigerator?

Incorrect answer: Open the refrigerator, put in the elephant and shut the refrigerator.

Correct answer: Open the refrigerator, take out the giraffe, put in the elephant and close the door. This question tests your forward planning.

3 The Lion King is hosting an animal conference. All the animals attend except one. Which animal does not attend?

Correct answer: The elephant. The elephant is in the refrigerator! This tests if you are capable of comprehensive thinking.

OK, if you did not answer the last three questions correctly, this one may be your last chance to test your qualifications to be a professional.

4 There is a river where the crocodiles live. How would you cross it?

Correct answer: Simply swim through it. All the crocodiles are attending the animal meeting! This question tests your reasoning ability. So ...

Results

- If you answered four out of four questions correctly, you are a true professional. Wealth and success await you.
- If you answered three out of four, you have some catching up to do but there's hope for you.
- If you answered two out of four, consider a career cooking hamburgers in a fast-food joint.
- If you answered one out of four, try selling some of your organs. It's the only way you will ever make any money.
- If you answered none correctly, consider a career that does not require any higher mental functions at all, such as law or politics.

2 SECOND CONDITIONAL

GRAMMAR QUICK CHECK
See p 56

1   We use the second conditional to talk about imaginary situations in the present or future and their results. For example, Peter has seen an advertisement for a job that he would really enjoy, but it requires an MBA, which he doesn't have. He says:

If   I *had* an MBA,   I *would*   *apply* for that job.
If   + past tense   *would*   + infinitive

2   We often use *were* instead of *was* in the *if* clause, especially in the advice structure: *If I were you …*

3   Do NOT use *would* in the *if* clause: *If I ~~would have~~ an MBA …*

3 OTHER CAREERS

Using your own ideas, think of the main differences between your life now and write sentences about what your life would be like if you were the following:

1   a doctor
If I was a doctor, I wouldn't have so much free time.

2   a stockbroker
_____

3   a politician
_____

4   a teacher
_____

5   a sports coach
_____

6   an actor
_____

7   a long-distance truck driver
_____

8   unemployed
_____

4 THIRD CONDITIONAL

GRAMMAR QUICK CHECK
See p 56

We use the third conditional to talk about imaginary events in the past and their results. For example, Kevin Jones is at the station and has missed the train to work. The reason is that he left home late. He would say:

If   I *had left* home on time,   I *would have*   *caught* the train.
OR
If   I *had not left* home late,   I *would not have*   *missed* the train.
If   + past perfect   would(n't) have +   past participle

Resolving conflict

45

5 PRACTICE

Write one or two sentences about each of these situations, saying how things might have been different.

LUCKY BREAKS AND BAD MISTAKES

JAMES SHALFORD earned a great deal of money working for a big investment firm, but always said he would stop at 35 and go into movies, which he loved. However, when he reached 35, he decided to stay on at his company. At 45 he was laid off, but he was too old to start a new career.

If he had left when he said he
was going to, he would have had
a much better chance of making
a successful second career in
the movies.

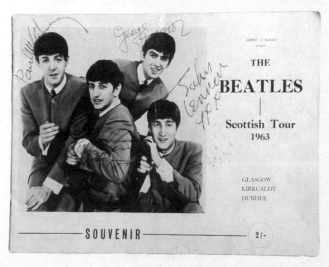

1   The Beatles' original drummer was a man called Pete Best. In 1962, shortly before the Beatles made their first recording, he left the group and was replaced by Ringo Starr.

_____

_____

2   In the 70s and 80s, a leading financier invested heavily in the stock market, and saw the value of his portfolio rise dramatically. In early October 1987, he sold all his shares and a few weeks later, stock markets around the world crashed.

_____

_____

3   When Anita Roddick was starting the Body Shop, she gave half of the company's shares to Ian McGlinn in return for an investment of a few thousand pounds. In a few years, the value of those shares rose to over £100 million.

_____

_____

4   Sometimes classmates can bring you luck. Paul Allen went to the same school as Bill Gates. In 1975, Gates asked Allen to join him in setting up a small new company called Microsoft.

_____

_____

Resolving conflict

6 WORDS THAT GO TOGETHER

Match the words in the list with the sets of verbs below. The word must go with *all* the verbs in a set. See the example.

a compromise	a concession	a deadline	a meeting	an agreement
money	pressure	schedule	time	

1
to make…
to cost …
to spend …   *money*
to save …

2
to look for …
to find …
to agree on …   _____

3
to waste …
to spend …   _____
to tell someone the …

4
to win …
to consent to …   _____
to agree to …

5
to reach …
to come to …   _____
to sign …

6
to hold …
to chair …   _____
to arrange …

7
to meet …
to work towards …   _____
to be up against …

8
to be under …
to apply …   _____
to feel under …

9
to be on …
to fall behind …   _____
to keep to …

7 PRACTICE

Use one of the expressions in exercise 8 above to complete these sentences. Make any changes that are necessary. Sometimes more than one answer is possible. See the example.

1 I thought the new car was $22,900 but with all the extras, it ended up _costing_ much more _money_ than I had expected.

2 I wanted Mrs Jones to work four days a week, but she only wanted to do two. In the end we _____ , and she now works for three days a week.

3 You have given them a bigger discount, generous repayment terms, and other benefits, and I think that we ought to try and _____ a few _____ in return.

4 The meeting went on for hours and hours, but the management and unions finally _____ and the strike was called off.

5 Yes, we do need to discuss this. Why don't you call my secretary and _____ – I think I am free most of next week.

6 Working for a newspaper like *The Times* can be stressful because you have to _____ every single day, and you cannot afford to miss one.

7 I have been _____ a lot of _____ at work, and my doctor thinks I need to take some time off to relax.

8 Things are going according to plan. We are currently _____ , and the project manager is confident we will finish on time.

8 VERBS FOLLOWED BY INFINITIVES OR *-ING* FORMS

GRAMMAR QUICK CHECK
See p 57

Some verbs and expressions are followed by an *-ing* form and others are followed by an infinitive. Complete the table by putting the words from the list in the correct column.

advise someone	*avoid*	*decide*	*enable someone*		*enjoy*
look forward to		*it's not worth*	*manage*	*risk*	*want*

A Common verbs and expressions followed by *-ing*:	**B** Common verbs and expressions followed by the infinitive:	
can't help	agree	seem
keep on	afford	threaten
consider	allow someone	would like
delay	arrange	_____
mind	need	
there's no point	offer	_____
	persuade someone	_____
_____	plan	
	prepare	_____
_____	promise	
	remind someone	
_____		
_____		
_____		

9 PRACTICE

Two colleagues at an air conditioner manufacturing company are talking about some negotiations that are taking place. Put the verbs in brackets into the *-ing* form or the infinitive. See the example.

A   How are the negotiations with Hellasco going?

B   It's not easy. They want ¹ _*to have*_ exclusive rights to sell our portable air conditioners in Greece, but I can't help ² _____ (feel) that it's a little early to grant them that.

A   They're still quite a new company, aren't they?

B   Yes, but they seem ³ _____ (be) very enthusiastic. And what they say is that if they had the exclusive rights, it would enable them ⁴ _____ (expand) much faster. They are planning ⁵ _____ (order) about ten thousand units next year but said they would consider ⁶ _____ (import) more if we allowed them ⁷ _____ (become) our sole distributors.

A   On the face of it, I wouldn't advise you ⁸ _____ (go) ahead with a concession like that. I mean, there's no point ⁹ _____ (cut) out all the other distributors unless you are sure you're doing the right thing. If they manage 10_____ (make) a success of it, fine, and I'm sure they would like 11_____ (have) the advantages of no competition – who wouldn't? But if it doesn't work, we risk 12_____ (lose) sales in an entire country and we can't afford 13_____ (let) something like that happen. Why is it worth 14_____ (take) a risk like that? What's in it for us?

B   That's what I need 15_____ (find) out. Anyway, I have arranged 16_____ (see) them again on Friday, and I'll ask what they would be prepared 17_____ (offer) us in return.

A   OK, but my feeling is that if you can delay 18_____ (come) to an agreement like that, so much the better. Go on 19_____ (talk) by all means, but I think we need a lot more information before we decide 20_____ (make) them our sole distributors.

10 OPEN SENTENCES

Complete these sentences about yourself and your work and put the verbs you use into the *-ing* form or the infinitive.

1   In my line of work, you can't avoid _____

2   I am really looking forward to _____

3   In the near future I have arranged _____

4   When I have time off, I enjoy _____

5   I have decided _____

6   As far as my career goes, I would like _____

7   It's not worth _____

8   I can't afford _____

Read the text and complete the exercises that follow.

WORKING ACROSS CULTURES

ALTHOUGH the idea of a 'national culture' or 'company culture' can seem a little vague and hard to define, it is possible to analyse cultures by seeing how they differ. One of the most extensive pieces of research into cultural differences was carried out by Geert Hofstede, while he was working for IBM in Holland. After [1]_____ the data from over 100,000 surveys in 40 countries, he worked [2]_____ that there were four main areas of differences which had an [3]_____ on the way people did business.

1 Individualist or collectivist societies

In an individualist society, people are only expected to [4]_____ after themselves or their family. In a collectivist society, people are seen as part of a tightly-[5]_____ group, which expects them to be [6]_____ and loyal in return for lifelong protection. The USA and the UK are clear examples of individualist societies, whereas Japan and Spain are collectivist societies.

2 Power and distance

Another important difference relates to the way power is shared between bosses and subordinates. French and South-East Asian managers have considerably more power than their subordinates and are reluctant to [7]_____. German and British managers, however, [8]_____ to give a greater degree of independence to their employees.

3 Masculinity/femininity

'Masculine' cultures favour individuals who are ambitious, and assertive. They also value people who can take the [9]_____ and who desire to get [10]_____ by doing a job well. Japan, and to a lesser extent Italy, are examples of this kind of culture. 'Feminine' cultures [11]_____ other things as valuable – they are characterized by looking for agreement and compromise, concern for personal relationships and the environment, and individuals are encouraged to look [12]_____ each other. Scandinavian countries and France have very strong 'feminine' characteristics.

4 Uncertainty/avoidance

In some cultures, individuals feel threatened by unknown situations and their [13]_____ goal is to reduce risks. These cultures try to control the future and can be authoritarian. Japan, France, Italy and Austria all show a high degree of uncertainty avoidance. They are often bound by tradition and demand more detailed information before [14]_____ a decision. The USA, the UK, and Canada see things from a different [15]_____ and show a much lower degree of uncertainty avoidance. In these countries, people are less cautious and are more prepared to take risks.

Resolving conflict

Choose the best option for each of the blanks.

1	**a** fetching	**b** gathering	**c** picking	**d** holding
2	**a** out	**b** off	**c** over	**d** on
3	**a** impact	**b** impression	**c** imprint	**d** onset
4	**a** hear	**b** see	**c** watch	**d** look
5	**a** tied	**b** glued	**c** knit	**d** locked
6	**a** omitted	**b** remitted	**c** submitted	**d** committed
7	**a** delegate	**b** divide	**c** spread	**d** authorize
8	**a** lean	**b** mean	**c** tend	**d** use
9	**a** start	**b** enterprise	**c** initiative	**d** beginning
10	**a** reward	**b** recognition	**c** recollection	**d** reception
11	**a** regard	**b** feel	**c** think	**d** believe
12	**a** forward to	**b** down on	**c** out of	**d** out for
13	**a** primary	**b** direct	**c** instant	**d** next
14	**a** doing	**b** making	**c** bringing	**d** arriving
15	**a** view	**b** opinion	**c** perspective	**d** attitude

Read the text and put the words in brackets into the correct form.

THE CORPORATE DIPLOMAT

In the world of mergers and acquisitions, the advice of management consultant Per Thorens is often sought by 1 _____ (worry) executives who want to avoid some of the mistakes that other companies have made. Thorens has always been 2 _____ (interest) in the way that differing cultures can lead to conflicts when companies merge, and he finds it 3 _____ (astonish) that many companies in the past used to have no clear strategies for dealing with the problems.

'Generally speaking, managers today are much more aware of the importance of cultures – and that's not 4 _____ (surprise) when you think about how many companies are going global. In my work I act like a kind of corporate diplomat – let's take an example. A big American corporation takes over a small Swedish manufacturer.

The Americans are all 5 _____ (excite) about the deal and want to make big changes, increase production and so on. The Swedes are all 6 _____ (convince) that that their jobs will disappear and they feel very 7 _____ (threaten). When I get to work, I try to get each side to communicate as much as possible, I go to each side and explain how the other feels, and I try and make them more aware of the other's culture. It's 8 _____ (amaze) what a difference something like good communication can make. Of course, things don't always go smoothly, and there are times when I can get very 9 _____ (frustrate), but on the whole, it's a very 10 _____ (fulfil) job.'

Resolving conflict

Grammar reference

SIMPLE TENSES

PRESENT SIMPLE

Form

The Present simple is formed from the infinitive. In the third person the verb ends in -s or -es.

AFFIRMATIVE	
I/you/we/they	work.
He/she/it	works.

QUESTION		
Do I/you/ we/they	work?	
Does he/she/it	work?	

NEGATIVE		
I/you/we/they	do not/don't	work.
He/she/it	does not/doesn't	work.

Use

1   We use the Present simple to talk about things that we consider to be permanent rather than temporary.
   Our new MD is Greek. She comes from Athens.
2   There are a number of verbs (called stative verbs) that are nearly always used in the simple form, not the continuous. The most common ones are:

believe	belong to	contain	depend on
doubt	guess	have (= possess)	
hear	imagine	involve	know
like	love	mean	own
possess	prefer	realize	seem
smell	sound	suppose	taste
understand	want.		

   Nearly everyone in this country has a mobile phone.

SIMPLE PAST

Form

The Simple past is formed by adding -d or -ed to the infinitive of regular verbs.

AFFIRMATIVE	
I/you/he/she/we/they	worked.

QUESTION	
Did I/you/he/she/we/they	work?

NEGATIVE	
I/you/he/she/we/they	did not (didn't) work.

Note: Many common verbs are irregular and need to be learnt. See the list on page 59.

Use

The Simple past is used to talk about finished events in the past. It is often used with past time expressions such as: *at 5 p.m., yesterday, last week, on Monday, last October, in 1987*, etc.
He got his first job with IBM in 1996.

CONTINUOUS TENSES

Form

The present continuous and past continuous are formed by using the verb *to be* and the *-ing* form of the verb:

PRESENT CONTINUOUS

AFFIRMATIVE	
I am/you are/he is/she is/ it is/we are/they are	working.

QUESTION	
Am I/are you/is he/is she/ is it/are you/are they	working?

NEGATIVE	
I am/you are/he is/she is/ it is/we are/they are	not working.

PAST CONTINUOUS

AFFIRMATIVE	
I was/you were/he was/she was/ it was/we were/they were	working.

QUESTION	
Was I/were you/was he/was she/ was it/were you/were they	working?

NEGATIVE	
I was/you were/he was/she was/ it was/we were/they were	not working.

Use

1   The continuous forms are used to talk about something in progress at a particular point in time:
*At the moment I **am driving** down Park Lane, and I'm going past a Mercedes showroom.*
*I **was talking** on my mobile phone when I had the accident.*

2   The continuous forms are used when we want to suggest that something is temporary rather than permanent.
*I **am working** at McDonalds, but I'm really a law student.*
*I met Anna during the university holidays when I **was working** at McDonalds.*

PERFECT FORMS

PRESENT PERFECT

Form

The Present perfect is formed by using the verb *have* and the past participle.

AFFIRMATIVE		
I/you/we/they	have	worked.
He/she/it	has	worked.

QUESTION		
Have	I/you/we/they	worked?
Has	he/she/it	worked?

NEGATIVE		
I/you/we/they	have not	worked.
He/she/it	*has* not	worked.

Use

1   We often use the Present perfect when there is a link between the present and the past.
*Mr Jackson is not here at the moment. He **has gone** to lunch.*

2   We often use the Present perfect to talk about experience, particularly with the words *ever* and *never*.
***Have** you ever **used** this computer?*
*No, **I've** never **seen** it before.*

3   The Present perfect is often used to talk about very recently completed events, especially with the word *just*.
*I'm thrilled. **I've** just **heard** that we have won the contract.*

4   The Present perfect is often used in unfinished time periods (e.g. *so far today*, *this week*, *yet*, etc.)
*That's the third complaint we **have had** this week, and it's only Tuesday.*

5   The Present perfect is often used with *how long*, *for*, and *since* and stative verbs (see above) to talk about duration.
*How long **have** you **known** Mr Jackson?*
*We **have been** colleagues for over ten years.*

6   We do **NOT** use the Present perfect with past time expressions like *yesterday*, *at 5.30*, *on Wednesday*, *last week*, *in December*, *in 1997*, *ago*, etc.

PAST PERFECT

Form

The Past perfect is formed by using *had* and the past participle.

AFFIRMATIVE		
I/you/he/she/it/we/they	had	worked.

QUESTION		
Had	I/you/he/she/it/we/they	worked?

NEGATIVE		
I/you/he/she/it/we/they	had not	worked.

Use

We use the Past perfect in the same way as the Present perfect, except that there is a link between an event in the past and a previous event. Compare the following with the examples above.

> Mr Jackson wasn't there. He **had gone** to lunch.
> She asked if I **had used** the computer.
> I said I **had never seen** it before.
> I was thrilled. I **had just heard** that we had won the contract.
> It was the third complaint that we **had had** that week, and it was only Tuesday.
> She asked how long I **had known** Mr Jackson.
> I said we **had been** colleagues for over 10 years.

PERFECT CONTINUOUS FORMS

PRESENT PERFECT CONTINUOUS

Form

The Present perfect continuous is formed by using *have/has been* + the *-ing* form of the verb.

AFFIRMATIVE		
I/you/we/they	have	been working.
He/she/it	has	been working.

QUESTION		
Have	I/you/we/they	been working?
Has	he/she/it	been working?

NEGATIVE		
I/you/we/they	have not	been working.
He/she/it	has not	been working.

Use

The Present perfect continuous is normally used with *how long, for*, and *since* to talk about the duration of a current activity.

> Here comes the train at last. I **have been waiting** for nearly forty minutes.

PAST PERFECT CONTINUOUS

Form

The Past perfect continuous is formed by using *had been* + the *-ing* form of the verb.

AFFIRMATIVE		
I/you/he/she/it/we/they	had	been working.

QUESTION		
Had	I/you/he/she/it/we/they	been working?

NEGATIVE		
I/you/he/she/it/we/they	had not	been working.

Use

The Past perfect continuous is used in a similar way to the Present perfect continuous, except that it is one stage back in the past.

> When the train finally arrived, I **had been waiting** for nearly forty minutes.

REFERRING TO THE FUTURE

We can refer to the future in a number of different ways.

GOING TO

1 We use *going to* to talk about plans and intentions.
> George is going to resign. He has had enough.

2 We use *going to* in predictions based on firm evidence.
> This is the biggest traffic jam I have ever seen. We are going to miss the plane.

WILL

1 We use *will* to talk about predictions.
> Over the course of the next two years, unemployment **will** fall gradually and inflation **will** remain constant.

2 We use *will* for spontaneous decisions.
> A: Oh no, I've got so much to do.
> B: **I'll** give you a hand with the filing if you like.

3 We use *will* in requests and offers.
> **Will** you make sure Mrs Harding gets a copy of this report please?

PRESENT CONTINUOUS

We use the Present continuous to talk about appointments and arrangements.
*The Sales Manager **is coming** to see me at 3.30 this afternoon.*

ACTIVE AND PASSIVE FORMS

Form

All the tenses have active and passive forms. The passive forms of the most common tenses are as follows:

TENSE	ACTIVE	PASSIVE
Simple present	I drive	I am driven
Present continuous	I am driving	I am being driven
Simple past	I drove	I was driven
Past continuous	I was driving	I was being driven
Past perfect	I had driven	I had been driven
Present perfect	I have driven	I have been driven
'will' future	I will drive	I will be driven

Use

In general, we use the passive when we want to focus on what happens, rather than on who is doing something. So for example, we can say:
*The letter **was posted** to you on Friday.*
(The focus is on the letter.)
instead of
*I **posted** the letter to you on Friday.*
(The focus is on the fact that I did it.)

CONDITIONAL FORMS

THE ZERO CONDITIONAL

Form

In the zero conditional, both parts of the sentence use the present tense.
*If prices **rise**, sales **fall**.*

Use

We use the zero conditional when the word *if* means the same as *when* or *every time*.

THE FIRST CONDITIONAL

Form

In the first conditional, the verb in the *if*-clause is in the present tense, and the other verb is in the future with *will*.
*If **I get** this promotion, my salary **will rise** by twenty per cent.*

Use

We use the first conditional to talk about the results of a situation that we see as a real possibility.

Note: Instead of *will*, we can use *may*, *might*, *could*, or the imperative.
*If the candidate **gets** here early, she **may want** to have a look around.*
*If the candidate **gets** here early, **let me know** at once.*

THE SECOND CONDITIONAL

Form

In the second conditional, the verb in the *if*-clause is in the past tense. In the other part of the sentence, we use *would* + infinitive.
*If I **had** a year's holiday, I **would travel** round the world.*

Use

We use the second conditional to talk about the results of situations that are imaginary or which we do not see as a real possibility.

THE THIRD (PAST) CONDITIONAL

Form

In the third conditional, the verb in the *if*-clause is in the past perfect. In the other part, we use *would have* + past participle.
*If we **had won** that contract, we **would have made** a great deal of money.*

Use

We use the third conditional to talk about the imaginary results of events that did not take place.

MIXED CONDITIONALS

Form

A common form of mixed conditional uses the past perfect in the *if*-clause and *would* + infinitive in the other part.

If **I had stayed** on at the company, **I wouldn't be** my own boss now.

Use

This is used to talk about the present result of an imaginary past event that did not take place.

GERUNDS AND INFINITIVES

A number of verbs and expressions are usually followed by the *-ing* form, and some are followed by the infinitive.

1   Common verbs and expressions usually followed by the *-ing* form are:

avoid	carry on	keep on
consider	delay	deny
dislike	enjoy	finish
can't help	involve	it's no use
look forward to	mind	miss
need (= passive meaning)		practise
risk	suggest	there's no point

   *I look forward to **hearing** from you.*

2   Prepositions are followed by the *-ing* form rather than the infinitive.

   *If you want to get on in Personnel, you have to be good **at dealing** with people.*

3   Common verbs and expressions followed by the infinitive include:

afford	agree	arrange	decide
deserve	expect	guarantee	hope
learn	manage	offer	plan
prepare	pretend	promise	refuse
seem	tend	want	would like

   *We don't seem **to have** them in stock.*

4   Expressions using *be* + adjective are normally followed by the infinitive:

   *It's easy **to make** mistakes.*
   *This manual is difficult **to understand**.*

COUNTABLE AND UNCOUNTABLE NOUNS

COUNTABLE NOUNS

Some nouns are countable. They have singular and plural forms.

a chair	*two chairs*	*three chairs,* etc.
an office	*two offices*	*three offices,* etc.

–   With singular countable nouns we can use the following words and a singular verb:

DETERMINER	NOUN	VERB
a/an		
an		
the	*office*	*is*
this		
that		
my/your/his/her/our/their		

–   With plural countable nouns we can use the following words and a plural verb:

DETERMINER	NOUN	VERB
the		
these		
those	*offices*	*are*
my/your/his/her/our/their		
some		
any		
many		
how many …?		
a few		
a lot of		

UNCOUNTABLE NOUNS

Some nouns are uncountable. They have no plural form.

the information (but we **cannot** say *two informations, three informations,* etc.)
the advice (but we **cannot** say *two advices, three advices,* etc.)

Some of the most common uncountable nouns are:

advice	machinery	accommodation
money	baggage	money
cash	news	equipment
progress	furniture	room (i.e. space)
information	traffic	luggage
weather		

many items of food and drink – rice, bread, sugar, meat, beer, water, wine, etc.

– With uncountable nouns we can use the following:

DETERMINER	NOUN	VERB
the		
this		
that	furniture	is
my/your/his/her/our/their		
some		
any		
much		
how much …?		
a little		
a lot of		

MODALS OF OBLIGATION

MUST, HAVE TO, AND HAVE GOT TO

These all express strong obligation. *Must* is often used when giving orders and in official communication, notices, etc. *Have to/have got to* is often used when you are talking about an obligation.
You **must** finish that report before you go home.
I'm going to be late. **I've got to** *finish a report before I can go home.*

MUSTN'T, CAN'T, NOT ALLOWED TO

These express prohibition. *Mustn't* is often used when giving orders and in notices, and *can't/not allowed to* are used when talking about something that is forbidden.
Cars **must not** *be left unattended at any time.*
*Sorry, you can**'t** park here. You are**n't allowed** to park here.*

SHOULD AND OUGHT TO

These express mild obligation, and are often used when giving advice.
You don't sound well – you **should** *see a doctor.*

NEEDN'T AND DON'T HAVE TO

These express a lack of obligation.
You can come to the meeting if you like but you **don't have to** *if you'd rather do something else.*

VOCABULARY

MAKE AND DO

The following words and expressions are used with *make*:

an appeal	an appointment	an attempt
a change	a claim	a comment
a contribution	a decision	a difference
a fuss	an impression	a loss
a mistake	money	a noise
a phone call	a profit	a promise
progress	a remark	a speech
a start	a suggestion	up one's mind

The following words and expressions are used with *do*:
engineering, law (e.g. study it)
a course (in US English: *take a course*)
everyday tasks – do the filing, do the washing up, do the accounts, etc.
a good job
military service
one's best
some more work
someone a favour
well

MULTIWORD VERBS

English has a lot of multiword verbs that are made up of a verb and small words like *up, on, to, into, back,* etc. They're common in spoken English, particularly in informal settings.
Please **go on**. (continue)
She **heads up** *our chemicals division.* (leads)
We won't **put up with** *this any longer.* (tolerate)

When you're learning a new multiword verb, pay attention to whether it can be separated or not.
Some can be separated:
He **turned down** *our offer.* (rejected)
OR *He* **turned** *our offer* **down**.

Some **can't** be separated:
Could you **look into** *this problem?* (investigate)
BUT NOT ~~Could you **look** this problem **into**?~~
Notice what happens to these verbs if we use a word like *it* or *them*.
He **turned** *it* **down**.
BUT NOT ~~He **turned down** it~~.

COMMON IRREGULAR VERBS

Infinitive	Past tense	Past participle
be	was	been
bear	bore	born
beat	beat	beaten
become	became	become
begin	began	begun
break	broke	broken
bring	brought	brought
build	built	built
buy	bought	bought
catch	caught	caught
choose	chose	chosen
come	came	come
cost	cost	cost
cut	cut	cut
deal	dealt	dealt
do	did	done
draw	drew	drawn
drink	drank	drunk
drive	drove	driven
eat	ate	eaten
fall	fell	fallen
feed	fed	fed
feel	felt	felt
fight	fought	fought
find	found	found
fly	flew	flown
forbid	forbade	forbidden
forget	forgot	forgotten
freeze	froze	frozen
get	got	got/gotten (US English)
give	gave	given
go	went	been/gone
grow	grew	grown
have	had	had
hear	heard	heard
hide	hid	hidden
hit	hit	hit
hold	held	held
hurt	hurt	hurt
keep	kept	kept
know	knew	known
lay	laid	laid
lead	led	led
learn	learnt	learnt
leave	left	left
lend	lent	lent
let	let	let

Infinitive	Past tense	Past participle
lie	lay	lain
lose	lost	lost
make	made	made
mean	meant	meant
meet	met	met
pay	paid	paid
put	put	put
quit	quit	quit
read	read	read
ride	rode	rode
ring	rang	rung
rise	rose	risen
run	ran	run
say	said	said
see	saw	seen
sell	sold	sold
send	sent	sent
set	set	set
shake	shook	shaken
shoot	shot	shot
show	showed	shown
shrink	shrank	shrunk
shut	shut	shut
sing	sang	sung
sink	sank	sunk
sit	sat	sat
sleep	slept	slept
speak	spoke	spoken
spend	spent	spent
split	split	split
spread	spread	spread
stand	stood	stood
steal	stole	stolen
stick	stuck	stuck
swim	swam	swum
take	took	taken
teach	taught	taught
tear	tore	torn
tell	told	told
think	thought	thought
throw	threw	thrown
understand	understood	understood
wake	woke	woken
wear	wore	worn
win	won	won
withdraw	withdrew	withdrawn
write	wrote	written

Answer key

1 EXCHANGING INFORMATION

1 Getting information

2 What does your company do?
3 Where is the company based?
4 Why are you learning English?
5 How long have you been studying English?
6 What do you do?
7 How long have you been working for them?
8 What are you responsible for?
9 Why are you doing this course?
10 Are you enjoying it?

2 Grammar quick check

2 We *have* progress meetings every Monday.
3 Sorry, you can't speak to the Manager at the moment – he's *talking* to a client.
4 The boss is away this week, so *I am running* the sales team.
5 The Internet *is becoming* more and more important in business.
6 *I've been working* for BT for six months.

3 Practice

1 need	7 arranges
2 is changing	8 comes
3 am travelling	9 have been setting up
4 think	10 am not having
5 don't understand	11 come
6 talk	12 speak

4 On a mission

2 b   3 e   4 f   5 c   6 a

5 Grammar quick check

a   the words in italics are all verbs in the *-ing* form
b   prepositions

6 Practice

No set answers

7 Vocabulary

1 efficient	6 unprofitable
2 private	7 parent
3 well-run	8 medium-sized
4 expanding	9 multinational
5 dynamic	10 old-fashioned

U	M	E	D	I	U	M	S	I	Z	E	D	E
W	N	R	T	Y	G	J	H	B	D	F	Y	R
E	X	P	A	N	D	I	N	G	F	F	N	W
A	A	P	R	I	V	A	T	E	D	I	A	A
S	L	W	S	O	S	F	R	E	W	C	M	F
A	G	E	F	F	F	E	D	F	R	I	I	G
P	R	L	E	D	R	I	S	D	E	E	C	F
M	U	L	T	I	N	A	T	I	O	N	A	L
S	N	R	V	F	H	T	Y	A	L	T	R	G
W	R	U	P	A	R	E	N	T	B	O	P	U
U	T	N	G	T	F	R	M	N	K	L	F	R
P	O	L	D	F	A	S	H	I	O	N	E	D

8 Set phrases: *make* and *do*

a   *make*: a complaint, a suggestion, money, a decision, a mistake, a noise, progress, an effort, a phone call
do: military service, a job well, some research, a lot of damage, someone a favour, the cleaning

b   2 making a very strange noise
3 do some more research
4 made a mistake
5 make a phone call
6 do me a favour
7 make money
8 did a lot of damage
9 make a suggestion
10 make a complaint

9 Grammar quick check

	BOOK	BOOKS	ADVICE
a/an	✓	–	–
six, seven	–	✓	–
my	✓	✓	✓
the	✓	✓	✓
this	✓	–	✓
these	–	✓	–
how much	–	–	✓
how many	–	✓	–
some	–	✓	✓
a little	–	–	✓
a few	–	✓	–
any	–	✓	✓

10 Practice

DIALOGUE 1

1 help	6 a few
2 some	7 machines
3 some	8 a little
4 equipment	9 some
5 is	10 a few

DIALOGUE 2

1 information	6 are
2 is	7 jobs
3 is	8 is very little
4 is	9 work
5 areas	10 many

11 Question time (some variation is possible)

2 What is teak used for?
3 Is there a strong demand for tropical hardwoods?
4 Is the price of teak rising?
5 Where does it all come from?
6 How quickly does teak grow?
7 How many years do you have to wait before the first harvest?

12 Checking understanding (sample answers only)

2 teak farming has a good future
3 demand is rising
4 a single log costs $20,000
5 should/ought to do something to replace the teak that we use
6 (you mean that) it grows quite quickly

13 The language of presentations

2 That brings me to my next point about
3 Let's turn to
4 I'm going to be talking about
5 As you can see from this graph
6 I'd like to begin with

14 Vocabulary review

1 b   3 d   5 d   7 c   9 d
2 b   4 c   6 b   8 b   10 a

2 SHARING IDEAS

1 Making suggestions

a 1 c 2 f 3 e 4 b 5 a 6 d
b (some variation is possible)
  2 It might be an idea to travel economy class.
  3 Why don't we open a branch in Spain?
  4 How about seeing Mr Jason now and Mr Hayes some other day?
  5 We'd better not be late for the meeting.
  6 I don't think we should offer a bigger discount.
c No set answers

2 Grammar quick check

No answers

3 Talking about processes

1 is done   8 are added
2 doesn't exist   9 checks
3 are carried out 10 publishes
4 do   11 are solved
5 is sent   12 is granted
6 describes   13 takes
7 is given   14 costs

4 Reading

a 1 D 2 C 3 A 4 B 5 E
b 1 F 2 T 3 F 4 F 5 F 6 T 7 F 8 F 9 T 10 T

5 Passive review

1 are used
2 is being developed
3 was invented by Chester Carlson
4 has never been changed
5 should be patented
6 will be transformed

6 Reacting to ideas

2 could   7 idea
3 before   8 How
4 don't   9 doing
5 won't   10 a try
6 explain

7 Evaluating ideas

a 1 d,g   3 c,h
  2 b,f   4 a,e
b No set answers

8 Grammar quick check

No answers

9 Practice

1 comes, will/'ll give
2 would apply, spoke
3 were, would/'d make
4 would/'d enjoy, had
5 stopped, would not/n't have
6 would you keep on, won
7 aren't, will/'ll get
8 carry, will/'ll make

10 *For* and *against*

No set answers

11 Vocabulary

1 executive   5 agree   9 brainstorming
2 shares   6 responsible 10 about
3 manual   7 better   11 agenda
4 fill   8 worth

Key word: chairperson

12 The language of meetings

a 1 E 2 F 3 B 4 D 5 A 6 C
b Anna
c 1 E 2 A 3 D 4 B 5 C 6 F

3 TACKLING PROBLEMS

1 Reading

3	done	7	set	11	cost
4	sent	8	grew	12	brought
5	began	9	held	13	came
6	gone	10	caught	14	built

2 Grammar quick check

No answers

3 Practice

a 2 met, was attending
3 got, were moving
4 decided, was not selling
5 were you doing, called
6 noticed, was checking
b No set answers

4 Company histories

a A 2 B 5 C 1 D 3 E 4
b 1 founded   6 had started
    2 had discovered   7 persuaded
    3 had married   8 had set
    4 took   9 had fought
    5 allowed   10 created

5 Causes and results

No set answers

6 Grammar quick check

No answers

7 Talking about current problems

2 You have missed the flight.
3 Your tickets haven't arrived yet.
4 I have lost my keys.
5 We have run out of catalogues.
6 We have redesigned our website.
7 It has cleared up.
8 Twenty people from the IT department have been made redundant.

8 Simple past or Present perfect?

1 have already reached
2 joined
3 came
4 Have you ever worked
5 hasn't finished
6 have gone
7 haven't spoken
8 haven't seen
9 broke
10 spent

9 Discussing mistakes

2 You should have used Hamlin Hire.
3 You shouldn't have accepted a quote like that.
4 I should have asked you first.
5 They should have put it up yesterday.
6 They should have thought of that before.
7 They should have phoned me this morning.

10 *Must, musn't,* or *needn't*

1	mustn't	3	needn't	5	must
2	must	4	must	6	mustn't

11 Vocabulary: *say* and *tell*

1	say	4	told	7	tell
2	tell	5	tell	8	tell
3	tell	6	said		

12 Vocabulary

2	employer	12	asset
3	entitled	13	recruit
4	benefits	14	encouraged
5	training	15	problems
6	salaries	16	communication
7	perks	17	budgets
8	discount	18	turnover
9	sharing	19	equals
10	staff	20	motivated
11	culture		

13 Rules and regulations

No set answers

14 Changing plans

2	can	7	fixed	11	fine
3	about	8	busy	12	me
4	come	9	meeting	13	if
5	make	10	say	14	No
6	Would				

15 Request, offers, and invitations

2 you mind coming
3 you mind if I come
4 you like to arrange
5 you mind bringing
6 you like to cancel

16 Politely does it (sample answers only)

1 Could you tell me when the next train to Kyoto leaves?
2 Would you mind coming back later?
3 I'm afraid that I'm a stranger here myself.
4 Excuse me, do you know if there is a cash machine near here?
5 Could you tell me how to get to Olympia from here?

4 PLANNING AHEAD

1 Talking about plans

a 1 C   2 B   3 D   4 A

b
2 is planning to
3 is expected to
4 is due
5 intends to
6 wants to
7 is going to
8 is about to
9 is hoping to
10 doubt

2 Plans and intentions

No set answers

3 Quiz: famous wrong predictions

1 d   2 c   3 b   4 e   5 f   6 g   7 a

4 Talking about probabilities

a
1 browsing
2 portals
3 download
4 animations
5 high-definition

b
1 definitely won't
2 probably won't
3 could
4 are likely to
5 will certainly

5 The language of predictions: practice

2 … will certainly develop alternatives to petrol
3 … are likely to lose their jobs because of new technology
4 … might rise later in the year
5 … is not likely/is unlikely to succeed

6 Writing

No set answers

7 Talking about probabilities

a
1 climbed steadily, went up gradually
2 fluctuated wildly
3 crashed, fell dramatically
4 rocketed, rose dramatically
5 fell gradually

b

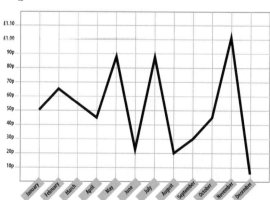

8 Reading

a
2 pre-tax
3 down-market
4 high-margin
5 large-scale
6 cut-price
7 well-managed
8 fast-growth
9 duty-free
10 long-term

b (sample answers only)

Strengths: large, profitable, cheap, well-managed, dynamic

Weaknesses: position of its London airport, seen as aggressive, poor public image, bad at handling customer complaints

Threats: air crash, unforeseen government regulations, competition from other cut-price airlines

Opportunities: new continental routes, possible increase in low-cost passenger numbers to 15%, cost reductions from Internet, advertising revenue from Internet

9 *If, when, in case, until*

1 b   2 a   3 d   4 e   5 c

10 Practice

a
2 … unless the lawyers have had a good look at it.
3 … won't make a profit unless we sell more than 100,000 units.
4 … go home until I have finished my work.
5 … phone you when I get to London.
6 … accept the job if they offer it to me.
7 … if we can sort these problems out.
8 … to work until the strike is over.
9 … when he calls in.
10 … in case the banks are shut when you get to Moscow.

b No set answers

11 Vocabulary

2 d   3 d   4 b   5 c   6 a   7 a   8 c   9 d   10 b
11 a   12 a   13 d   14 c   15 d

5 RESOLVING CONFLICT

1 Quiz
No set answers

2 Grammar quick check
No set answers

3 Other careers
No set answers

4 Grammar quick check
No set answers

5 Practice (sample answers only)
1 If he hadn't left the group, he'd be very rich now.
2 If he hadn't sold his shares, he would have lost a lot of money.
3 If Anita Roddick had kept the shares, she would be even richer now.
4 If he hadn't gone to the same school as Bill Gates, he wouldn't have been so succcessful.

6 Words that go together
2 a compromise	5 an agreement	8 pressure
3 time	6 a meeting	9 schedule
4 a concession	7 a deadline	

7 Practice (sample answers)
2 agreed on a compromise
3 win ... concessions
4 came to an agreement
5 arrange a meeting
6 meet deadlines
7 under ... pressure
8 on schedule

8 Verbs followed by infinitives or -ing forms
Words followed by -ing:

avoid	enjoy	look forward to
it's not worth	risk	

Words followed by infinitive:

advise someone	decide	enable someone,
manage	want	

9 Practice
2 feeling	9 cutting	16 to see
3 to be	10 to make	17 to offer
4 to expand	11 to have	18 coming
5 to order	12 losing	19 talking
6 importing	13 to let	20 to make
7 to become	14 taking	
8 to go	15 to find	

10 Open sentences
No set answers

11 Reading and vocabulary
1 b 2 a 3 a 4 d 5 c 6 d 7 a 8 c 9 c 10 b
11 a 12 d 13 a 14 b 15 c

12 Adjectives ending with -ing and -ed
1 worried	5 excited	9 frustrated
2 interested	6 convinced	10 fulfilling
3 astonishing	7 threatened	
4 surprising	8 amazing	